D1446081

The British Labour Party and Defense

THE WASHINGTON PAPERS

... intended to meet the need for an authoritative, yet prompt, public appraisal of the major developments in world affairs.

President, CSIS: David M. Abshire

Series Editor: Walter Laqueur

Director of Publications: Nancy B. Eddy

Managing Editor: Donna R. Spitler

MANUSCRIPT SUBMISSION

The Washington Papers and Praeger Publishers welcome inquiries concerning manuscript submissions. Please include with your inquiry a curriculum vitae, synopsis, table of contents, and estimated manuscript length. Manuscript length must fall between 120 and 200 double-spaced typed pages. All submissions will be peer reviewed. Submissions to *The Washington Papers* should be sent to *The Washington Papers*; The Center for Strategic and International Studies; 1800 K Street NW; Suite 400; Washington, DC 20006. Book proposals should be sent to Praeger Publishers; One Madison Avenue; New York, NY 10010.

The Washington Papers/153

The British Labour Party and Defense

Bruce George

with

Timothy Watson
and Jonathan Roberts

Foreword by Robert E. Hunter

Published with The Center for
Strategic and International Studies
Washington, D.C.

PRAEGER

New York
Westport, Connecticut
London

Library of Congress Cataloging-in-Publication Data

George, Bruce.
    The British Labour Party and defense / Bruce George, with Timothy
Watson and Jonathan Roberts.
      p. cm. – (The Washington papers, ISSN 0278-937X ; 153)
    Includes bibliographical references and index.
    ISBN 0-275-94201-5 (alk. paper). – ISBN 0-275-94202-3 (pbk.)
    1. Great Britain – Military policy. 2. Labour Party (Great
Britain) 3. Nuclear weapons – Great Britain. I. Watson, Timothy.
II. Roberts, Jonathan. III. Title. IV. Series.
UA647.G39 1991
355′.0335′41 – dc20   91-30287

The *Washington Papers* are written under the auspices of The Center
for Strategic and International Studies (CSIS) and published
with CSIS by Praeger Publishers. The views expressed in these papers
are those of the authors and not necessarily those of the Center.

British Library Cataloging-in-Publication data is available.

Library of Congress Catalog Card Number: 91-30287
ISBN: 0-275-94201-5 (cloth)
       0-275-94202-3 (paper)

First published in 1991

Praeger Publishers, One Madison Avenue, New York, NY 10010
An imprint of Greenwood Publishing Group, Inc.

Printed in the United States of America

The paper used in this book complies with the Permanent
Paper Standard issued by the National Information Standards
Organization (Z39.48-1984).

10 9 8 7 6 5 4 3 2 1

92-1274

Contents

Foreword

The fortunes of political parties can never be divorced from the times. For historians, struggles over policy or principle can seem quaint, indeed almost incomprehensible to observers who already know the outcome of both debate and events. This is particularly true about debates over foreign policy, where domestic political argument is often less about the nation's own future than about perceptions of external events, perhaps beyond the control of the country in question. Generally, however, this clear-sighted retrospective does not occur for years if not generations, as in, for example, a backward look at isolation's effects on domestic U.S. politics between the world wars or the British Tory Party's internal battles over appeasement. Even the Democratic Party's divisive arguments over the Vietnam War did not become clearly recognizable for many years as a major source of the party's difficulties in mobilizing an effective contest for the presidency. To this day, the split within the party over foreign and defense policy has not been fully healed.

For Americans, it is particularly instructive to look at the roughly parallel experience found in the evolution of the British Labour Party of the past two decades. Britain did not occupy the center stage of world events as did the United States; there was no national trauma comparable to Vietnam (Suez had a profound impact because it dealt with the decline of Britain's global role, and the Falklands War, exploited by a master politician, merely intensified the political difficulties already facing Labour). But Britain's Labour Party, even more than the U.S. Democratic Party, found that its electoral fortunes, its philosophical center of gravity, and even its composition of leadership—with major defections to a new Social Democratic Party—were deeply affected by disputes over foreign and defense policy.

There is an ironic quality to these disputes today; the international basis for the struggle—the cold war in political content, nuclear weapons in policy instruments—has undergone profound change quite independent of domestic political competition in Britain or the philosophical debate and leadership struggle in the Labour Party. To an extent far greater than the U.S. Democratic Party and more comparable to Germany's Social Democratic Party, Labour is still deeply affected by the legacy of debates that have lost most of their contemporary value. Whether Britain renounces its nuclear status—an issue that can still produce warm discussion—has become essentially irrelevant, except in some less-than-central aspects of the future of European security or the character of the European Community.

But the Labour Party's debates over the cold war, relations with the United States (in particular), and "the bomb" are not, in fact, ancient history or now simply beside the point. The same leaders occupy top positions; indeed, the man who led Labour to a basic review of its defense policy, Neil Kinnock, is the party's leader most likely to become prime minister since the dominant rule of Margaret Thatcher began in the 1970s. The roles of the Parliamentary Labour Party, the constituency parties, the unions, and such factions as Militant Tendency are still in major part the products of these obsolescent debates. They remain interesting not as historical artifacts but as examples of the continuing dynamics of the British Labour Party and as clues to what it might do when returned to power.

In explaining the Labour Party's debates in recent years over foreign and defense policy, Bruce George has few peers. A member of Parliament since 1974, he has been on the firing line in party debates. He was also one of the senior members of the party who chose to remain and to pursue his objectives from within—paraphrasing Hugh Gaitskell, to "fight and fight and fight again." This is thus compelling history; it is also invaluable insight into the workings of a major Western political party, whose fortunes have risen steadily in recent years in part because of the reviving quality of debates fought and won, such as that surrounding the defense issue.

Bruce George originally wrote this essay for a CSIS project on British attitudes toward nuclear weapons, conducted during 1987–1988. That project is long since past, its insights overtaken by the march of history. But the analysis and discernment of George's contribution, updated in the summer of 1991 to account for later developments, remain pertinent, and it is a sure guide to the evolution of the British Labour Party.

Robert E. Hunter
Vice President, Regional Programs
Director, European Studies
Center for Strategic and International Studies
September 1991

Acknowledgments

The authors thank Rosemary Reilly, Catriona McDonald, Simon D'Albertson, Tim Lister, and Josh Arnold-Foster for their contributions to this study.

About the Authors

Bruce George has been a Labour Member of Parliament since February 1974. He has been a Member of the House of Commons Defence Select Committee since its inception in 1979 and is now Ranking Labour Member; he is also general rapporteur and former chairman of the North Atlantic Assembly's Political Committee. Bruce George has been a frequent contributor to *Jane's Defence Weekly* and has edited *Jane's NATO Handbook* since 1989. He has written and lectured very extensively on security issues, specializing in NATO, UK defense policy, Mediterranean security, and East-West relations.

Timothy Watson is a parliamentary research assistant to Bruce George and was special assistant for *Jane's NATO Handbook 1990-91* and *1991-92*.

Jonathan Roberts, a former parliamentary research assistant to Bruce George, was deputy editor of *Jane's NATO Handbook 1990-91*.

Summary

This volume examines the evolution of the British Labour Party's defense and security policies since the party's formation in 1900. It concentrates on the last decade, which has witnessed a gradual transformation from unilateral nuclear disarmament and the removal of U.S. nuclear bases from UK soil to retention of the British nuclear deterrent and support for NATO's new nuclear and conventional strategies. The latter position has been held by the party throughout most of its postwar history.

The authors examine in detail how defense policy, in particular nuclear disarmament, was Labour's Achilles' heel in the 1983 and 1987 general elections and how the party fundamentally transformed its defense and security policies after its third successive election defeat. According to the authors, the early 1980s were an aberration in defense and security policies. Changes in the international environment have spurred Labour to reexamine its policies in this area and to realize that these policies would condemn the party to eternal opposition. As a result, Labour now has a pragmatic set of defense and security policies relevant to the 1990s, as evidenced by the party's robust position on the Gulf War, its support for Britain's nuclear deterrent, and its welcome of the "London Declaration" following the NATO summit in July 1990.

In a speech to the Royal United Services Institute in London during the Persian Gulf War, Labour Party leader Neil Kinnock spelled out the party's new policies: "Security for the nation is the prime duty of any government and, apart from the obligations of domestic security, government must make its best contribution to international security by alliance where appropriate, by agreement where possible and by deterrence when necessary." This new approach, the authors contend, gives Labour a set of defense and security policies that need not be feared by NATO, the United States, or the British electorate.

The British
Labour Party
and Defense

1

The Labour Party

This volume traces the evolution of the British Labour Party's defense and security policies since the party's creation in 1900 and examines the labyrinthine process of decision making in this policy sphere. It also assesses how these policies may affect the party's chances of winning upcoming general elections.

For the 91 years since the party's formation, Labour has held office without recourse to other parties on four occasions — 1945–1951, 1964–1966, 1966–1970, and 1974–1979. Until the past few years, its likelihood of achieving office again was questionable. The era of Margaret Thatcher came to a dramatic conclusion in November 1990. There followed a rapid movement by the Conservative Party back toward the middle ground of British politics, a position Labour had been holding for several years. During the 1980s, both parties had abandoned the center, but a combination of events has drawn the parties much closer together across a range of policies. In no area has this been more marked than in defense.

After the party's defeat at the 1987 general election, three well-known analysts wrote, "It is no exaggeration to say that the result of the next General Election . . . could well be decided on . . . the [Labour] Party's defence policy."[1]

1

The Changing Political Scene

The recent period has arguably been one of the most eventful in postwar British politics. When 1990 began, the Labour Party led the Conservative government by 12 to 15 percentage points in the opinion polls. Throughout the remainder of the year, the Conservative government's popularity continued to decline, particularly with the implementation of the poll tax that replaced domestic rates as the form of taxation for local government. The Conservative government also suffered sensational by-election defeats — particularly in Mid-Staffordshire and in Eastbourne, where previously huge Conservative majorities were reversed by opposition parties.

When early autumn brought continuing government unpopularity, a worsening economy, and Prime Minister Margaret Thatcher's almost total isolation in the European Community, Michael Heseltine, her former defense secretary, decided to challenge her for the leadership of the Conservative Party. Although Thatcher defeated him on the first ballot, she had been severely wounded, and within 48 hours of the result's being declared, she announced her intention to resign. The way was opened for other Conservative Members of Parliament (MPs) and cabinet ministers to challenge Heseltine. Douglas Hurd, the foreign secretary, and John Major, the chancellor of the exchequer, announced their decisions to do so within minutes of Thatcher's resignation. On November 27, 1990, John Major was elected prime minister by his fellow Conservative MPs, and within 24 hours had formed his first administration.

With their fortunes briefly transformed by Major's election, the Conservatives led in the opinion polls for the first time in 18 months. This lead, however, was due more to a honeymoon period for Major than to a change in the public's attitude toward Conservative Party policies. By March 1991, the two main parties were once again more or less even in the opinion polls.

At this writing, it is uncertain whether defense will be as important an issue in the next election as it was in 1983 and 1987. Even if the government did decide to raise the defense and security issue, it would be hard to exploit it, because of Labour's stance during the Persian Gulf War. The war may have been the final piece in the jigsaw puzzle bringing the party back to a political consensus in defense matters. Speaking in the House of Commons on January 15, 1991, Neil Kinnock stated:

> From the outset of this crisis caused by the aggression of Iraq against Kuwait, it has been clear that, in the interests of the whole world community, the will of the United Nations must prevail and Iraq must quit Kuwait completely and unconditionally. It is also clear that great devastation would result from a war. It would therefore be best, if at all possible, for the purposes of the United Nations to be achieved without further use of force, with sanctions and the blockade being the maximum time to have effect.
>
> It is plainly the case, too, that if it should become certain that the objectives of the United Nations can be achieved only by the use of armed force against Iraq, as authorised by Security Council resolution 678, such force would then have to be used.
>
> . . . When I vote tonight I shall vote in the same way and for the same reasons as I have done since our first debate on 7 September. I shall continue to be consistent with the objectives that I set out then and which were adopted by the Labour Party at their conference. I shall act to ensure that neither Saddam Hussein nor anyone else can represent the subtleties of voting in this House of Commons in this democracy as being in any way a concession to his aggression. I shall vote in support of the United Nations because, for all our sakes, the purposes and authority of the United Nations must prevail.[2]

A number of world developments have made Labour's new policy far more attractive and relevant — particularly the improved relationship between the two superpowers and blocs, the Intermediate Range Nuclear Force (INF) Treaty, and the possibility of further nuclear and conventional arms control treaties as well as unilateral conventional cuts. Both superpowers are sharply reducing their defense budgets so that more can be done for their domestic economies. This is especially true of the Soviet Union, which is experiencing serious internal problems. The North Atlantic Treaty Organization (NATO) has calculated that the Soviet Union is now unable to launch a surprise conventional attack against it. Not only have Eastern bloc states turned away from communism during the past 18 months, but also Soviet troops are withdrawing from their erstwhile satellites. The former Warsaw Pact can no longer be regarded as a substantial military threat to NATO. The reunification of the two Germanys, the reduced perception of threat, and such treaties as the Conventional Armed Forces in Europe (CFE) and Strategic Arms Reduction Talks (START) will seriously affect the force structures of the NATO allies and the Soviet Union and may result in significant further adjustments to those forces in the near future.

To analyze a party's security policy and to predict changes in that policy require an awareness of the party's status in government or opposition; the relationship between party ideology and pragmatism; the international situation (particularly the state of East-West relations); and the state of relations between Britain and the United States and Britain and the Soviet Union. The balance of power within the party and between the parties must also be examined. One must examine the views of the leadership, domestic political and economic considerations, public opinion (although it should be noted that the Labour Party has often ignored public opinion when drafting policy), and the windows of opportunity that open when some or all of these factors align. Following its third consecutive general election defeat in 1987, the Labour leadership, conscious that many of its policies, particularly defense, had been deeply unpopular, instigated a full policy review that took two years to complete.

The new policy on defense has been produced at a very crucial juncture in the electoral calendar. The next general election certainly will take place by the middle of 1992. It is, therefore, a most opportune moment to examine the current policy, its evolution, its relationship to the traditional attitude toward defense and the unilateralism of the 1980s, and the probable content of the security policies to be presented to the electorate at the next election. How controversial a policy will it be? Will the Conservative Party's defense policy or Labour's be more appropriate to the situation in Europe in 1992? Will the economy be more of an issue than defense?

In examining these policies, this volume will explore the principles underlying Labour's defense and foreign policies since the party's formation in 1900; the structure of the party, which affects the decisions emanating from it; and those aspects of Labour's nine decades of history that are relevant to an understanding of its attitude and actions toward Britain's defense.

Labour's security policies of the past 10 years, its transition to a non-nuclear defense stance in the period following the 1979 parliamentary election defeat, and the forces that have directed that evolution will also be analyzed. The crucial question Labour faced when reviewing its defense policy post-1987 was whether some or all of the unpopular policies previously adopted on defense ought not to be abandoned or modified. The monograph will also examine the pressures that existed to maintain the status quo or to shift away from those policies so strongly rejected by the public in the past two parliamentary elections.

**Foreign and Defense Policy:
Philosophy and Practice**

For many decades before the birth of the Labour Party, the conduct of Britain's external relations was guided by traditional foreign policy, which included promoting British national interests, defending Britain's imperial and commercial network, and managing a European balance of power to ensure Britain's security. This policy was enforced as neces-

sary by the use of the British army, or, more frequently, by
the navy's gunboat diplomacy.[3] The policy emerged from
considerations of British geography, national independence, and prevailing economic and strategic needs.

All British governments followed that accepted policy.
Britain's military might resulted in a stable international
system and contributed to a century of relative peace in
Europe, lasting from 1815 until World War I. Foreign policy
and defense issues rarely figured in elections, largely because of the continuity of foreign policy from one government to another. These issues were not considered in detail
in Parliament because of secret diplomacy and a practice of
decision making by a narrow elite.

> In British politics the decline of "continuity" in foreign
> policy irrespective of electoral change was not seriously
> challenged until the appearance of the Labour
> Party. . . . with the rise of the Labour Party to a posi-
> tion of political effectiveness the first real protest was
> made against the removal of foreign affairs from popu-
> lar or party control.[4]

Labour viewed traditional foreign policy as selfish class
politics. It characterized traditionalism as immoral power
politics and arrogant imperialism, designed to advance the
interests of the capitalist ruling class. Labour wanted nothing to do with traditional policy, rejecting it in the name of
superior morality and intellectual understanding. The party was determined to establish, as Ramsay MacDonald put
it in 1911, "a well thought-out and constructive policy" of
its own.[5]

Labour proposed to transform international relations
by conducting the nation's foreign policy according to socialist principles. It wanted to create an international system that embodied the socialist objectives of economic
organization, social justice, fraternity, and cooperation. Labour's goal of social reconstruction required that it not
waste resources by waging war when those resources could

be used more effectively in Britain. Party members believed that a wise and pacific foreign policy would lead to a reduction in arms spending, thus leaving more funding for social programs and industrial reform at home. Traditionalist foreign policy hindered the achievements of the domestic socialist movement.

The principles of Labour's foreign and defense policies were derived from nineteenth-century radicalism and working-class internationalism. Nineteenth-century radicals were largely pacific and humanitarian. They were suspicious of all foreign policy entanglements and foreign powers and believed that the size of the armed forces should be kept to a minimum. Rather contradictorily, Labour also considered Britain the champion of liberty against tyranny and the supporter of peoples struggling to free themselves from foreign and domestic oppression.

The British Labour Party sought to provide a more positive approach to international peace. Its aim was to democratize foreign policy and abolish secret diplomacy. Labour wanted to see Parliament control foreign policy and fully debate and vote on all treaties before committing Britain to any binding agreements. This process would remove suspicion, jealousy, and rivalry from foreign policy. It would also allow the Labour Party to publicize its peace program. Later, however, when the governments of Clement Attlee, Harold Wilson, and James Callaghan made decisions about nuclear weapon systems, all three prime ministers refused to confide in more than a few of their ministerial or parliamentary colleagues.

From its beginning, Labour's documents, election manifestos, and leaders' speeches have reflected consistent themes in foreign and defense policies. Despite this philosophical continuity, the party has often had difficulty fulfilling its ideals when confronted by the realities of governing. Labour is by no means unique among European socialist parties in this respect.

M. R. Gordon has identified four of Labour's ideological themes: internationalism, international working-class soli-

darity, anticapitalism, and antipathy toward power politics.[6] Other principles include a distrust of power blocs and
alliances; low priority for defense expenditure; dislike of, if
not revulsion for, nuclear weapons; a commitment to the
rule of law; and a distaste for war combined with a commitment to arms control and disarmament.

From its inception, the Labour Party has displayed antipathy toward power politics. It has objected to the use of
force to settle disputes on the grounds that force is immoral
and inexpedient and leads to war. If nations would trust one
another, then troops would not be needed. World War I
proved to the Labour Party and others that the existing
world order was profoundly unsafe. By 1918, Labour was
calling for a League of Nations and for a system of collective security based on the rule of law. This theme can still
be found in party documentation and pronouncements. The
1918 election manifesto called for "a peace of International
Co-operation."[7] That call was followed four years later by
demands for "an all-inclusive League of Nations with power
to deal with international disputes by methods of judicial
arbitration and conciliation."[8] The demand for collective security was repeated in all manifestos until 1935, despite
Hitler's rearmament of Germany.

By 1945, the socialist-radical tradition in security had
been badly tarnished. In the space of 30 years, the spirit of
socialist internationalism had twice been let down. Most
socialists in northern Europe, particularly Labourites, acknowledged that well-armed collective security was the only acceptable alternative to isolated and vulnerable neutral-
ity. The 1959 manifesto pledged Labour's support to the
United Nations (UN), but acknowledged that

> power is required to make the rule of law effective. That
> is why during the period of east-west deadlock we have
> stood resolutely by our defensive alliances and contrib-
> uted our share to western defence through NATO
> [North Atlantic Treaty Organization]. It is our view
> that any weakening of the alliance would contribute to
> a worsening of international relations.[9]

This tradition of reliance on international institutions is still alive and well, as illustrated by Labour's appeal for UN intervention in the Falklands War and by their specific support for the UN resolutions against Iraq.

The assumption that international working-class cooperation would prevent war was undermined by World War I, when virtually every European socialist party voted to support its government's war effort. According to David Caute,

> The record of the European Left in International Affairs is one of ambivalence and ambiguity, of confusion and contradiction. . . . that the left is by nature and without exception internationalist and anti-patriotic is a common belief which dissolves into dust on the most cursory examination of the evidence.[10]

The overwhelming majority of the Labour Party endorsed the British war effort. Despite its frequently repeated antimilitarism, the party loyally supported national efforts in both world wars and joined the governing coalitions during those conflicts. In manifestos issued following World War I, World War II, and the Korean War, Labour invariably and legitimately claimed to have played an important role in the success of the war effort.

Historically, other socialist parties have also had difficulty reconciling the ideal of international brotherhood among working people with the recognition that, in a world of competing states, self-protection is imperative. Labour's particularly slow and painful process of coming to terms with nationalism and patriotism, however, sets it apart from most other European socialist parties; few could question the patriotic credentials of leaders such as Felipe Gonzalez, François Mitterrand, Andreas Papandreou, or Gro Harlem Brundtland.

Although the Labour Party is internationalist and belongs to a number of socialist organizations such as the Socialist International, its fellow parties abroad have not always considered it to be in the mainstream of international socialist cooperation. From its inception, the Labour Party has been somewhat marginalized in the international democratic socialist movement.

The 1918 Labour Party constitution established the goal of a socialist society in Great Britain. Capitalism was seen as the source of all economic, political, and social wrongs. In practice, however, the Labour Party has endorsed a mixed economy, especially while in government. For much of its history, Labour has enjoyed close relations with the arch-capitalist society, the United States, although there has almost always been a segment of the party that consistently condemned the United States.

The United States is seen as both the largest democracy and the center of the twin vices of capitalism and commercialism. Several Labour leaders have had close relationships with U.S. presidents, however, especially with Democrats such as Franklin Roosevelt, Harry Truman, Lyndon Johnson, and Jimmy Carter. Prime Minister James Callaghan wrote in his autobiography *Time and Change* that, as foreign minister, he found "Mr. [Edward] Heath's deep and lasting commitment to Europe had weakened our relations with the United States, and as a strong believer in the Atlantic Alliance, I was determined that these must be strengthened."[11] Callaghan later, as prime minister, had a good relationship with President Carter. Labour's relations with U.S. presidents reached a new low in the 1980s, but currently the Labour leadership is striving hard to undo the damage and the memories of that period.

In July 1990, Neil Kinnock visited President Bush in Washington. On his return to London, Kinnock stated that "there are no differences at all between us in the areas we discussed." Moreover, President Bush described the meeting as "a good exchange of views" as well as "very rewarding and amicable." The Gulf conflict also vividly highlighted the improving relationship between the Labour Party and the U.S. administration. Throughout Iraq's occupation of Kuwait and the subsequent war to liberate the country, the Labour leadership consistently supported the stance taken by President Bush and the UN. Speaking in the House of

Commons on January 17, 1991, Neil Kinnock echoed the President's view that the war began on August 2, 1990, when Iraq invaded Kuwait—not the previous night when the allied air offensive began.

The Labour Party has displayed a similar ambivalence toward Russia and the Soviet Union, despite early manifesto commitments to support the then new Soviet state. In the 1930s the party became disillusioned with the Soviet Union as a result of Joseph Stalin's totalitarian state and was highly critical when the Soviets signed the pact with Nazi Germany in 1940. The relationship changed again in 1941 when Hitler invaded the Soviet Union. By the end of the war, the Soviet Union was seen as a friendly defender of democracy, having fought hard and sacrificed much in the war against Germany. By the late 1940s, with the division of Europe and the cold war, however, the Soviet Union was again viewed with extreme suspicion.

The fear of electoral consequences, a perception of being too close to the revolutionary Soviets, contributed to Labour's ambiguous position. The 1922 manifesto contained an explicit denial of any revolutionary tendency in the British Labour Party, concluding that

> democratic government can be made effective in this country without bloodshed or violence. Labour's policy is to bring about a more equitable distribution of the nation's wealth by constitutional means. This is neither Bolshevism nor Communism, but common sense and justice.[12]

The Labour Party remains in the tradition of European social democracy that emerged from a rejection of Marxist socialism. Immediately after World War II, the European Left split. This split allowed the social democratic parties to support NATO because they were defined, in part, as anti-Communist. That anticommunism became an integral part of the British Labour Party's defense and foreign policy.

With the onset of the cold war, Labour governments

seemed unable or unwilling to live up to their pure principles of socialist foreign policy. While in government from
1945 to 1951, Labour united with the United States against
the Soviet Union. This dichotomy between principle and
reality has continued to the present. As Patrick Seyd
writes:

> The neutralist segment identified with the 1950s re-
> mained significant in the 1970s. On the one hand the
> Left was critical of American foreign policy, especially
> its involvement in South-East Asia and its interven-
> tion in the domestic affairs of Chile in 1973. On the
> other hand the Left's hostility towards the Soviet
> Union was greater than in the 1950s. . . . The Left held
> a view of the Soviet Union, distinct from that of the
> right, which influenced its view of defense policy re-
> quirements. . . . [It argued] that the Soviet Union was a
> status quo power concerned more with the consolida-
> tion of territory than expansion, that military expan-
> sion in NATO member countries would create internal
> problems for the Soviet leadership and that ideological
> confrontation, perpetuated by the Soviet leadership,
> was more concerned with maintaining internal stability
> within the Soviet bloc than with external aggression.
> The Left therefore argued that Britain should take a
> lead in reducing arms expenditure since this would re-
> duce international tensions and would not be exploited
> by Soviet aggression.[13]

A segment, though fast diminishing, of the party still
regards the pure socialist ideals as relevant. In 1981, the
party's National Executive Committee (NEC) produced a
discussion document entitled "A Socialist Foreign Policy,"
indicating that the early principles of foreign policy were
far from extinct: "In a world threatened by depression and
war, internationalism is no longer a dream, but a necessity.
We need to co-operate with the international labour movement if we are to build a democratic socialist society in

Britain."[14] But the Labour Party has moved far from its early 1980s posture, as will be discussed later.

The Labour Party has, then, found it difficult to reconcile the practicalities of foreign policy with socialist principles. As Peter Byrd has written, "Defense policy has always been an uncomfortable policy arena for the Labour Party."[15] It is much easier to be idealistic in opposition than in the front line of governmental decision making. The perceived gulf between stated goals and performance exists not only in the sphere of foreign policy but also in domestic, economic, industrial, and social policy. The failure of Labour governments to execute policies devised in opposition and their apparent sacrifice of socialist foreign policy ideals have been, and will remain, a source of constant difficulty and intraparty conflict.

Decision Making

It is important for political scientists and analysts, domestic and foreign, to comprehend the process by which decisions are made by any government or political party. It is crucial when examining a socialist party, not only because the process reflects the balance of forces and ideologies that shape the party's decisions, but also because the party structure itself has a profound effect on those decisions and on the policy-making process. When Labour was founded in 1900, there was no specific working class representation in Parliament. The Parliamentary Labour Party (PLP) became the legislative arm of the external party, and only gradually did its leadership in Parliament assume a greater significance.

The structure, organization, and culture of the Conservative Party favor a strong party leader. In the Labour Party, those factors tend to work against a strong leadership. The Labour Party is a pluralistic organization with numerous centers of influence: the party conference, the PLP, trade unions, the NEC, the party bureaucracy, and the shadow cabinet (if in opposition) and cabinet (if in government).

The Party Conference

Labour, like many other social democratic parties, bestows great power on extraparliamentary bodies. Although many leaders have tended to have great difficulty in making and executing decisions, Neil Kinnock has established his authority. The Labour Party, because of its organizational structure, has been referred to as a "bottom-up" party, emphasizing the important contribution of the mass membership, exercised particularly through the annual party conference.

The annual conference is the governing body of the party outside Parliament. It includes nearly 3,000 delegates, who represent the constituency parties, affiliated trade unions, socialist societies, MPs, Members of the European Parliament (MEPs), and parliamentary candidates who attend in a nonvoting, ex-officio capacity. The party conference is constitutionally the primary policy-making body in the party and has ultimate authority over the NEC and the PLP. Policy is determined by party members who vote on resolutions submitted for debate by the NEC, trade unions, or Constituency Labour Parties (CLPs). Resolutions passed by a two-thirds majority become policy, which is promoted by the NEC and implemented by the PLP. The trade unions currently constitute an overwhelming 90 percent of the conference vote. For most of Labour's history, this majority has been welcomed by the leadership because it has provided solid support against the more radical constituency representation. At the 1989 conference in Blackpool, however, this most favored status was severely criticized, and there were calls for a sharp diminution of union dominance. The 1990 conference set in motion plans to reduce the trade union block vote from 90 percent of total votes cast at the conference to 70 percent.

The trade unions and CLPs have frequently presented radical defense resolutions at the conference. While Clement Attlee was prime minister from 1945 to 1951 and leader of the opposition from 1951 to 1955, his authority over the PLP and the conference was sufficiently strong to maintain the party's robust defense posture. Critical resolutions submitted at the conference were defeated with the aid of the union block vote. Attempts to eliminate conscription (1946, 1947, 1954, and 1955) were defeated regularly, as were calls for reviews of military commitments, but the leadership had to work hard to control the growing hostility toward nuclear weapons. On a card vote,* the 1955 conference defeated a call to place "on record its opposition to the manufacture of the hydrogen bomb and all other nuclear weapons by Great Britain and its condemnation of the Government's policy of using these weapons unconditionally in the event of war."[16]

Hugh Gaitskell had much greater difficulty containing the unilateralist tendencies. By 1960, he had lost control of the conference to the left wing of the party and its antinuclear policies. At the famous 1960 conference at which Gaitskell, before defeat, made his speech to "fight, fight, and fight again to save the Party we love," two resolutions on defense were carried on card votes. These resolutions asserted Labour's antimilitaristic views and emphasized the party's hostility toward nuclear weapons. They are a clear reminder of the party's original socialist principles and demonstrate the resistance within the party to the leadership's often more moderate policies:

> This conference considers that world peace and nuclear disarmament are imperative. The only defence for Britain is for the settlement of international differences by

---

*Each union representative votes for his union members by a card vote (held when a vote by show of hands is inconclusive). If his union has decided to oppose a policy and comprises 500,000 members, his "card" vote is equal to 500,000 people opposing the policy. The "for" and "against" are added up and expressed in total numbers "for" and "against" the adoption of a proposed policy. This system is under review.

negotiations and a spirit of toleration between the nations and an understanding that countries with different political systems can and must live with each other. Conference demands that the Government should press for an international agreement on complete disarmament, and in the meantime, demands the unilateral renunciation of the testing, manufacture, stock-piling and basing of all nuclear weapons in Great Britain.

This Conference believing that the great majority of the people of this country are earnestly seeking a lasting peace and recognising that the present state of world tension accentuates the great danger of an accidental drift into war, calls upon the Labour Party to make a clear declaration that a Labour government will, when returned to office, establish our defence and foreign policies on:

a) A complete rejection of any defence policy based on the threat of the use of strategic or tactical nuclear weapons;

b) The permanent cessation of the manufacture or testing of nuclear and thermo-nuclear weapons;

c) Patrols of aircraft carrying nuclear weapons and operating from British bases ceasing forthwith;

d) The continuation of the opposition to the establishment of missile bases in Great Britain;

e) A strengthening of the United Nations Organisation, including the admission of representatives of the Chinese Peoples Republic, with a view to the creation of a new world order and the avoidance of a return to the methods of the cold war period;

f) Pressing for the reopening of discussions between nations at the earliest possible moment as the means by which world disarmament and peaceful coexistence can be most readily achieved.[17]

The 1961 conference carried the resolution condemning "the establishment of Polaris bases in Great Britain," but strongly rejected the resolution demanding "a complete rejection of any defence policy based on the threat of the use of strategic or tactical nuclear weapons . . . [and] the permanent cessation of the manufacture or testing of nuclear and thermo-nuclear weapons."[18]

Although the Harold Wilson government of 1964–1970 continued the Polaris program and began its improvement, the party conference endorsed a reduction in defense expenditures and a cutback in commitments, especially those "out of area." It failed in its attempts to secure the British withdrawal from NATO, to remove the British Army of the Rhine (BAOR), and to halt the production of nuclear weapons. After Labour's 1970 defeat, the party moved to the left, although the leadership remained in the hands of the moderate Wilson-Callaghan wing of the party. The leaders wanted Britain to remain a nuclear power and were able to contain, albeit with difficulty, the pressure for substantial change. Labour governments promised, and more or less delivered, reductions in defense expenditures that brought Britain to the level of its major European allies. Above all, they committed themselves *not* to move toward a new generation of nuclear weapons.

In the defense debate at Blackpool in October 1988, Ron Todd, general secretary of the Transport and General Workers Union (TGWU), led the fight against the leadership and opposed any change of the status quo. The platform (officially sanctioned by the NEC) presented a compromise resolution, affirming "its commitment to the total elimination of all nuclear weapons in the world to be brought about by steps of unilateral, bilateral, and multilateral nuclear disarmament," supported the INF Treaty, reiterated its support for further arms negotiations, and condemned the Conservative government for both its purchase of the Trident submarine and its "obstructionist and isolationist stance, regardless of the progress being made towards nuclear disarmament by international effort."[19] The resolution, known as Composite 55, was supported by Neil Kinnock, but opposed by the TGWU and several smaller unions. It was defeated by a vote of 3,277 million to 2,942 million.

A "non-platform" (not officially put forward by the NEC) resolution, Composite 56, called for a campaign for unilateral removal of all nuclear weapons and bases from Great Britain. The party leadership opposed the motion, but it was carried by a vote of 3,715 million to 2,471 million. The TGWU voted its block of 1.25 million against the platform's resolution and in favor of unilateral disarmament. Composite 56 stated that "Labour's pledge to unconditionally remove all nuclear weapons and nuclear bases from British soil and waters in the first parliament of the next Labour government is one of the party's most important policy gains and a vital step towards nuclear disarmament worldwide."[20]

Of all the trade unions, the TGWU plays the most vital role in the Labour party conference; its vote currently represents one-twelfth of the total conference vote. Todd's speeches have had the effect in the past of weakening the leadership's efforts to modernize the party's platform and to reformulate defense policy. Robert Harris, writing for the *Observer*, called Todd's speech at a preconference, left-wing rally in 1989 a "treat for all connoisseurs of Labour fratricide."[21] Todd's actions also called into question a trade union leader's right to exercise such a profound influence. As the *Observer* pointed out on October 5, 1988, Todd's union and its large vote challenged Kinnock's ability to create flexible policy. As the newspaper commented, Todd was determined that the "policy review on defence is not to be allowed to succeed unless it reaches his union's chosen conclusion."

The National Executive Committee

The National Executive Committee bridges the gap between the PLP, a Labour government or shadow cabinet, and the party at large. Its 31 members normally meet once a month. This committee is very influential because it governs the party, conducts studies on salient issues, formulates policy statements, structures the agenda for the debate at conferences, and implements conference decisions.

The NEC is composed of the leader, deputy leader, 11 members elected by the trade unions, and 7 members elected by the CLPs. It must elect five additional women members. There is a single representative from each of the National Union of Labour and Socialist Clubs and the Young Socialists. At times, the NEC is dominated by the party leader, who is also prime minister if the party is in government. Under both the Wilson and Callaghan governments, the NEC made regular statements critical of the Labour government; even the left-wing party leader Michael Foot subsequently had difficulties controlling it. One of Neil Kinnock's achievements has been to secure a substantially supportive majority; his control over the NEC was consolidated by the conference elections in 1988 and 1989. When Kinnock prepared for the key phase of his policy review, he expected a majority of at least 20 votes in the NEC on most issues.

The NEC operates through an elaborate structure of committees and subcommittees, whose areas include domestic policy, international affairs, local government, and organization. The International Section of the policy directorate is responsible for all international contacts on behalf of the party. It provides staff support for the NEC International Committee and its policy review process. The International Committee is made up of 20 of the 31 NEC members.

Until recently a mass of subcommittees of the NEC were established to recommend policy. These groups were amorphous, almost uncontrollable organizations with a broad membership. They produced vast reports, which were difficult for the party to synthesize, and made recommendations to the NEC.

Former subcommittees investigating defense and international affairs have included the Defence Study Group, which was formed to examine current British defense policy, to develop proposals from which the Labour Party could form a socialist defense policy for Britain in the 1990s, and to produce a defense policy for a democratic socialist party. This study group tended to meet fairly regularly, usually in the House of Commons, and has been heavily biased toward the left. The subcommittees of the Defence Study Group have reported twice: first in 1977 and again in 1983. One subcommittee contributed to the 1981 NEC statement to the party conference, "Nuclear Weapons and the Arms Race" and to the party's 1982 program.[22]

Kinnock reformed this inherently chaotic process. The policy review process was conducted by seven committees with a restricted and controllable membership producing policies that fitted in more coherently with the way the party was evolving. The most recent endeavor, chaired by Gerald Kaufman MP, shadow foreign secretary spokesman, and Tony Clarke, a senior trade union official, was designated the "Britain in the World Committee." This committee was established to review international affairs and defense policy as part of the overall policy review begun after the 1987 election defeat. The first phase of the review was concluded at the party conference in October 1988. The second phase was submitted to the 1989 conference and passed by a show of hands.

The Parliamentary Labour Party

The parliamentary element of the Labour movement is the Parliamentary Labour Party (PLP), which is 228 strong (excluding the deputy speakers, who do not vote). The PLP has been more disciplined recently than in previous years and has been better controlled and managed by Kinnock than by any of his predecessors since Attlee.

Several committees within the PLP discuss defense matters, including the Labour Party Defence and Services Committee. The PLP also has a Foreign Affairs Committee. These bodies have a very limited influence on decision making; they are not intended to form policy, but are helpful for briefing MPs and may also be used as a sounding board by the leadership.

Until the early 1980s, the leader of the Parliamentary Labour Party was elected by the PLP. As a result of constitutional reforms at the 1980 conference, the leader is now chosen at the annual party conference by an electoral college that currently comprises 40 percent trade union representatives, 30 percent PLP representatives, and 30 percent CLP representatives. This broader electoral base gives enhanced authority to the leader, but it presents a common dilemma for the leadership: deciding whether to follow the apparent wishes of the mass membership or whether to shape policy according to its own perception of party interests. There have been occasions when a Labour leader has ignored the conference but at the risk of paying a high price.

The party is a complicated structure with many power centers. The leader often has difficulty imposing central control over the PLP and mass organizations, which frequently conflict. The late John Maxton MP once observed that "if a leader can't ride two horses at once, then he should not be in the bloody circus."[23] Indeed, straddling the two horses — the PLP and the general membership — has become a difficult and uncomfortable posture.

The party leader plays an important role in policy formulation. Attlee, Wilson, and Callaghan remained staunchly prodefense, pro-Alliance, and pronuclear, in part because of their personal experiences. (Major Attlee served in the trenches of World War I, and Callaghan was a humble seaman in World War II.) Michael Foot was a fervent unilateralist, and his leadership not only reflected the party's shift in that direction but also reinforced it. Neil Kinnock was confronted with a dilemma. Like his mentor, Michael Foot, Kinnock had been a lifelong unilateralist. He also wished to be prime minister. Critics argued that to make that ambition more achievable he had to make a decision between abandoning, or at least adjusting, his unilateralist position.

Kinnock had to become more flexible in his approach to security issues and to question his own views. It must have been an agonizing process for a man who once said that if he ever abandoned unilateralism, he hoped his wife would leave him and take the children with her. He had either to maintain his principles and probably face another electoral defeat as well as the likelihood of his personal return to the backbenches or reappraise his position. He decided upon the second course of action. The next few years will determine whether Kinnock's pragmatism will prevail over the commitment to the traditional goals of the Labour Party.

Intraparty Ideological Divisions

Labour's position on defense also depends upon which wing of the party dominates. There have always been ideological, personal, and institutional differences within the party, usually expressed through megaphone diplomacy; internal conflict in the Labour Party is neither unusual nor eradicable. The party's defense position in recent years was largely the product of the left's dominance. The new left also represents a generational change, which has important implications for defense and foreign policy.

The postwar left in Parliament was variously called "Keep Left," "Keeping Left," the "Bevanites," and the "Tribune Group." In more recent years the Tribune Group split into two: Tribune, the majority of whose members are designated "soft-left" (pro-Kinnock), and the Campaign Group, currently the "hard-left" faction of the party (probably now only 20 in membership). These leftist groups were highly critical of the United States, except for a brief period during the late 1940s and the emergence of the cold war.

The distribution of aid under the Marshall Plan and the Soviet Union's excesses led to a temporary reorientation, of which the late Richard Crossman wrote, "I had quite forgotten how unashamedly pro-American the *New Statesman*, *Tribune*, Miss Jennie Lee, Mr. Foot, and I were in those days."[24]

In the past few years, the once dominant center-right has coalesced into such organizations as "Labour Solidarity" and the "Manifesto Group." Defections to the Social Democratic Party (SDP) as well as resignation, deselection, and an influx of left-wing members after the last two elections have greatly diminished the strength of this wing of the party. This trend was exacerbated by some sudden "St. Paul-like conversions" to the now dominant Tribune Group. This shift has led to the disbandment of most of the center-right organizations. Recently, however, there has been some blurring of the difference between the center-right and soft-left, and both groups have rallied behind the current leadership. Neil Kinnock and his deputy, Roy Hattersley, were once designated "the dream ticket" precisely because they brought together the moderate-left and the center-right wings.

The split over defense roughly mirrored the divisions over ideology. According to Craig,

> the threat to our future rises directly as a result of United Kingdom membership of the North Atlantic Treaty Organization and [this conference] is resolved to commit the next Labour Government to . . . an immediate total and unilateral withdrawal from the North Atlantic Treaty Organization.
>
> Such a commitment is to be included in the next general election manifesto.[25]

Most factions have recently united behind the policy review. Some believe in traditional policy, some have been converted, and others are supporting for political reasons.

Labour defense policy is also affected by whether Labour is in government or in opposition. Peter Byrd has described Labour's government-opposition dichotomy, pointing out that policies developed in opposition are sometimes modified or even abandoned when the party is in government. This often provokes anguished cries of "foul" and "betrayal" from party activists.[26] In the past few years, constitutional amendments passed at the conference have sought to make it much more difficult to deviate from the path laid down by the conference.

The apparently inherent conflict between the party conference and a Labour cabinet is reinforced by the constitutional autonomy of the cabinet and the direct line of communication between the electorate and the government. This conflict raises the question of whether a Labour prime minister is ultimately responsible to the party or to the electorate. There has usually been a distinction between declared policy (dictated by the party conference) and operational policy (determined by practical constraints). Byrd notes, "Labour defence policy has always emerged from a difficult dialectical process between what is desired and what is possible."[27]

During the 1979 to 1983 and 1983 to 1987 parliaments, the party shifted to the left, a change reflected in its security policies. After a general election defeat, the party has tended to go through a period of self-evaluation. The party conference usually exerts a tighter grip on the PLP because the counterbalancing influence and facilities of the civil service and other domestic and international pressures are in suspended animation when the party is out of office. Nevertheless, the new realism after the 1987 election defeat meant that the leadership imposed a remarkable degree of influence over the conference, though not without either difficulties or cost.

International Influences

The Labour Party is also subject to international pressures. It belongs to a wide variety of international socialist organizations that are becoming increasingly interested and influential in the area of security, such as the Socialist International and its Disarmament Advisory Council (SIDAC).[28] Indeed, the European dimension has a fundamental influence upon the promotion of Labour's defense policies. The Labour Party needs the European socialist parties to be receptive to its defense policy. Over the past few years, as the party has become more European in outlook, it has adopted a more European approach to security and defense issues. Labour's statements on the INF Treaty were affected, for instance, by decisions the European socialist parties had made in March 1987.

In recent years, social democratic parties within NATO countries have established a number of bodies to bring about a more coordinated approach to security. One, SCANDILUX, was an interparty forum founded in 1980 by social democratic parties in the smaller Scandinavian and Benelux countries belonging to NATO. The French Socialists, the British Labour Party, and the Social Democratic Party of Germany (SPD) were active participants. The socialist and social democratic parties of member countries of the Atlantic Alliance, EUROSUD, and SCANDILUX have joined together to form EUROLUX in Europe, which stands for the "Meeting of Atlantic Alliance Socialist Parties."

Labour participates in the Confederation of Socialist Parties of the European Community (EC) and in the Socialist Group in the European Parliament. Although defense is excluded by the Treaty of Rome, which set up the EC, foreign policy, defense-industrial cooperation, and security matters are increasingly falling within the community's purview. As 1992 and the Single European Market approach, security will be ever more central to these discussions. In fact, EC socialists discuss defense matters as "security" rather than "defense," partly because defense is excluded from the treaty, but also because of Irish sensitivity on defense matters. All positions on security are worked out to please everybody. Socialist Members of Parliament attending the North Atlantic Assembly (NAA), the Western European Union (WEU), and the Council of Europe also meet to attempt to gain a degree of policy cohesion, although their success should not be overstated.

Other Sources

The Labour Party's security policy is influenced by a diverse body of intellectual thought, both institutional and individual, domestic and external. These sources have in-

cluded the Campaign for Nuclear Disarmament (CND) and
the peace movement as a whole; academic writers such as
Mary Kaldor, Edward Thompson, and Gwyn Prins; academic institutes such as the School of Peace Studies at
Bradford University; analysts within the Labour Party; the
PLP; party headquarters at Walworth Road; and journalists such as Duncan Campbell. In the past few years, CND
has been marginalized within the Labour Party, as indicated by the majority opposition to unilateralism at recent
party conferences and by the leadership supporting the use
of force in the Persian Gulf War.

In the 1980s a substantial and growing body of litera-
ture advocating alternative defense policies developed.
Much of the impetus for this came from outside the party,
from such sources as *Common Security* (1982), the disarmament program that resulted from a study by the Independent Commission on Disarmament and Security Issues,
known as the Palme Commission. This report contained the
opinions of a wide variety of security specialists from the
West, East, and South, and from all shades of ideological
opinion. The late Olaf Palme stated in his introduction: "It
is . . . of paramount importance to replace the doctrine
of mutual deterrence. Our alternative is common security. . . . The long-term goal . . . must be general and complete disarmament. . . . We propose the establishment of a
battlefield nuclear-weapon-free zone starting in central Europe."[29] Ironically, the only Labour MP on this commission,
Dr. David Owen, left the Labour Party before the report
was published.

The concept of "common security" is much in vogue
among social democratic parties and has been picked up
and exploited by the Soviet Union. Its goal is to eliminate
the destabilizing tendencies inherent in the current strategic balance by decreasing the possibility that either side
might be tempted to fight a limited nuclear war or acquire
a first-strike capability. Reasonable sufficiency—that is,
maintaining forces sufficient for defense but incapable of
winning an offensive war—would decrease the likelihood of

a military confrontation in Europe. Although the origins of common security are usually traced to the Palme Commission, one member of that commission, the SPD security specialist Egon Bahr, has done the most to develop the concept.

Much more work has been undertaken in the former Federal Republic of Germany (FRG) than elsewhere. The studies by West German academic institutes and peace research institutes as well as the policy outputs of the SPD itself are far more significant and influential in the area of security than the work done by any other socialist party.

The British contribution to the concept of common security and defensive defense can be seen in the research project undertaken by the Alternative Defence Commission (ADC), set up by the Lansbury House Trust. In the introduction to its report entitled *Defence without the Bomb*, Frank Blackaby of the Stockholm International Peace Research Institute (SIPRI) wrote:

> To say No to nuclear weapons is not a defense policy. The question that arises: if Britain does renounce nuclear weapons, what defense policy should it adopt? The remit of the Commission was to review a wide range of alternative non-nuclear defense policies for Britain. . . . The persons who were invited to serve on the Commission had one tenet in common; they all accepted the initial premise — that Britain should renounce the use, or deployment on its territory, of nuclear weapons.[30]

The commission contained a number of Labour Party members who were, at that time, prominent advisers to the Labour Party. More recently, the ADC has published a follow-on report, *The Politics of Alternative Defence: A Role for a Non-Nuclear Britain* (1982).

The Campaign for Nuclear Disarmament was founded during the 1950s. At times it has had a significant influence on the Labour Party, notably during the 1950s and again during the early part of the 1980s. It had an especially large role in the 1983 election. Many close ties link the party and the CND, and CND thinking has influenced the party's defense policy. After the 1983 election defeat, Labour attempted to distance itself from CND, and since then, the movement's influence on the party has been very limited.

Finally, an important network of bilateral and multilateral contacts between parties, leaders, parliamentarians, and—when in office—ministers also affects policy making. The NEC report to the 1988 conference revealed that the party has met with such prominent figures as David Lange, Labour prime minister of New Zealand; Gro Harlem Brundtland, Labour prime minister of Norway; Karoly Groz, prime minister of Hungary; Dick Spring, leader of the Irish Labour Party; Oskar Lafontaine, deputy chairman of the SPD; Michael Manley, leader of the People's National Party of Jamaica; Svend Auken, leader of the Danish Social Democratic Party; Ingvar Carlsson, Social Democratic Party leader and prime minister of Sweden. Defense issues also figured prominently in meetings between former SPD leader Johannes Rau and Neil Kinnock. Before the 1987 elections, Kinnock made two visits to the United States, where, on the second occasion, he met President Ronald Reagan for his allotted half-hour. Links with the German SPD are probably the strongest, however. The amount of research underpinning the SPD's security policy is worthy of commendation, and politicians such as Karsten Voigt and Egon Bahr are impressive in their own right. Much less original thinking has emerged from the Labour Party thus far.

The remarkable events that have taken place in the Soviet Union and Eastern and Central Europe since the mid-1980s have led the parties of both left and right to incline toward a greater degree of consensus in their defense and security policies. There is now arguably greater agreement between the policies of the British Labour Party and NATO than at any time since the late 1970s.

2

The Nuclear Dimension
of Security Policy

Labour in Government

The Labour Party held office from 1945 to 1951, from 1964 to 1970, and from 1974 to 1979. These Labour governments acquired a reputation for being soft on defense—a reputation largely unjustified, especially in the period up to 1979, as an examination of defense expenditures since 1945 will confirm. Since the first Attlee government until 1979, Labour governments had broadly supported a nuclear weapons policy in the context of cold war instability.

The formation of the Maud Committee in 1940 heralded the beginning of production of atomic energy and weapons. The following year Winston Churchill authorized the creation of the project that constructed an atomic bomb. With Britain then in a state of war, the whole process was shrouded in secrecy, and Parliament was not informed. Clement Attlee maintained this approach when he became prime minister in 1945.

In his biography of Attlee, Kenneth Harris wrote that before the Potsdam Conference, all Attlee knew was that the Americans were working on a new, different, and bigger kind of bomb, and he had deliberately refrained from trying to find out what progress was being made with it.[1] President Truman did write to Attlee on August 1, 1945, to say that the United States was about to explode bombs over Japan. Harris notes that

> Attlee did not demur. His information was that the Japanese would fight for at least six months, at a great cost of life to the Allies, and that victory over Japan could only be achieved by shifting American troops from Europe and thus further prejudicing the European balance of power in favour of Russia. If the bomb would end the war in six weeks rather than six months, Attlee was for it.[2]

After Hiroshima and Nagasaki, Attlee cabled Truman that Hiroshima had shown the world "that a new factor pregnant with immense possibilities for good and for evil has come into existence. . . . There is widespread anxiety as to whether the new power will be used to serve or to destroy civilization."[3] He proposed that they should "make a joint declaration of our intentions to utilize the existence of this great power, not for our own ends, but as trustees for humanity in the interests of all peoples in order to promote peace and justice in the world."[4]

The new Labour government continued to develop the atomic bomb and maintained an obsessive secrecy. Colin McInnes writes that

> there was a distinct feeling that nuclear weapons policy was something almost too terrible to talk about openly. As had been the case with Churchill, the full cabinet and Parliament were kept totally in the dark, and political control was left to a few senior figures.[5]

With the 1946 passage of the MacMahon Act, which prevented the United States from sharing information about the bomb, Britain proceeded autonomously to develop its own.

The MacMahon Act was the impetus for "the most important decision Attlee made in relation to atomic energy . . . that Britain should produce her own bomb." This decision was made on the advice of the British Chiefs of Staff.[6] Later, when the bomb's existence was publicly known, Attlee was criticized for developing an independent British deterrent.

Harris states, however, that one should judge the decision in the light of the prevailing international circumstances, notably the growth of the Soviet threat and the fear of U.S. isolationism, which, two years before the establishment of NATO, threatened to leave Britain exposed. Attlee also expressed his concern that if cooperation with the United States had been possible, "it might have left the UK [United Kingdom] entirely in the hands of the Americans."[7] He believed that for a "power of our size and with our responsibilities to turn its back on the bomb did not make sense."[8]

Harris argues that regardless of whether Attlee was correct in proceeding with the independent deterrent, he should be criticized for his secrecy. From 1945 to 1950 there was not a single Commons debate on atomic energy. "In his readiness to shroud in secrecy what Britain was doing about her bomb, [Attlee] connived at arrangements which were constitutionally dubious. Nearly all his cabinet were systematically kept ignorant."[9]

The prime minister had many other reasons for maintaining the high degree of secrecy. He wanted to avoid setting off anti-Americanism, and he was afraid that the opposition would embarrass the government if given any information on the state of British nuclear weapons.

Attlee wanted to avoid rousing the left wing of the party and mistrusted some of his cabinet; in an interview with the academician John Mackintosh, he said that some of his own cabinet "were not fit to be trusted with secrets of this kind."[10] In keeping the weapons secret, Attlee could also claim to be following the precedent Churchill had set during the war.

During the period of Labour government from 1945 to 1951, the significant decisions about nuclear weapons were made by two ad hoc cabinet committees. The first committee, "GEN 75," included Clement Attlee, Ernest Bevin, Herbert Morrison, Stafford Cripps, and (later) Arthur Greenwood and Hugh Dalton.

Attlee called it the atom bomb committee. Margaret Gowing, author of the seminal study of the British atomic and nuclear program, writes that for 18 months after the election, this committee was the only cabinet body responsible for atomic weapons. The second committee, "GEN 163," comprised Clement Attlee, Ernest Bevin, Herbert Morrison, John Wilmot, Christopher Addison, and Harold Alexander, but not Stafford Cripps or Hugh Dalton. It was GEN 163 that, in 1947, decided to proceed with the production of the atomic bomb. Gowing commented that this was "one of the most successfully executed programmes in British scientific and technological history."[11]

When Churchill became prime minister, he was surprised and pleased to see how far atomic weapons had been developed. Attlee had "done good" by stealth, which fueled left-wing resentment.

Churchill's government maintained much of the secrecy surrounding nuclear weapons, although the full cabinet discussed the decision whether to proceed with the next generation of nuclear weapons—the hydrogen bomb—three times between April and July 1954. The third meeting of the full cabinet resulted in the authorization to produce the hydrogen bomb. That meeting was "the first and last time that a British cabinet has been allowed to make the decision on a new generation of nuclear weapons."[12] Churchill was not prepared, however, to allow the Parliament to realize the true nature of Britain's nuclear weapon systems.

Despite the fact that Attlee's government, by producing Britain's atomic bomb, had paved the way for Churchill to authorize development of the hydrogen bomb, in 1955 the Labour Party declared its opposition to nuclear weapons and reaffirmed its policy of disarmament. The election manifesto declared

> Ultimately the menace of the H-bomb can only be removed by world disarmament, which covers all kinds of

weapons. We shall cooperate in any genuine plan for
effective international control, even though it involves,
as it must, sacrifices of national sovereignty.[13]

The manifesto added that, "as a first step, we believe that
Britain should propose the immediate cessation of H-bomb
tests."[14]

Labour was unable to effect this policy because the party remained in opposition until 1964. During that time,
Britain acquired hydrogen bombs, and after the United
States abandoned Skybolt, which he had wanted to procure,
Harold Macmillan decided that Britain should obtain the
U.S.-built, submarine-based Polaris missile system. Macmillan and John Kennedy's Nassau agreement to sell Britain the Polaris system was approved by the cabinet on January 3, 1963. It called for British submarines and warheads
with U.S. missiles. Thus, the "V-force" of Vulcan, Victor,
and Valiant bomber aircraft, which were semideployed in
the 1950s and carried hydrogen bombs after 1961, was the
first and last truly homemade British deterrent. This fact
became important in 1964, when the Labour Party chose to
make the independence of the Polaris program a major issue in its election campaign. Before the election, the Labour
Party had been highly critical of the Nassau agreement and
pledged to renegotiate.

Shortly after the election, the Labour government decided to continue the Polaris program, although with four,
not five, submarines. The decision was made by three members of the cabinet: Harold Wilson, who was prime minister; Patrick Gordon Walker, foreign secretary; and Denis
Healey, defense secretary. Harold Wilson was at pains to
point out that the decision was made prior to the famous
Chequers meeting. He wrote:

In the first days of the new government in October
1964, I had discussed with Patrick Gordon Walker and
Denis Healey the future of the Polaris project in the
light of the information now available to us. It was well

past the point of no return; there could be no question
of cancelling them except at inordinate cost. We decided to go ahead with four of the projected five submarines, and to ensure their deployment as a fully committed part of the NATO defence forces. There was to
be no nuclear pretence or suggestion of a go-it-alone
British nuclear war against the Soviet Union. This decision was endorsed by the Cabinet Defence Committee, later by Cabinet, and was, therefore, not under review at Chequers.[15]

Others felt that Denis Healey's eloquence that weekend at the prime minister's country residence, Chequers,
swayed the leading ministers, civil servants, and chiefs of
staff and was instrumental in the fundamental revision.
This thorough review made sweeping recommendations for
the security policy of the Labour governments from 1964 to
1970. The Labour government opposed the idea of the multilateral force (MLF) and maintained its high commitment
to NATO.

Harold Wilson proposed an "Atlantic nuclear force" that
was to be under NATO control, but the concept was abandoned. Subsequently, this Labour government was reluc-
tantly compelled to plan and partly implement British military withdrawal from the most important of its bases "East
of Suez." Under the inspired leadership of Denis Healey, it
was decided to reorganize defense decision making by es-
tablishing a unified Ministry of Defence headed by a single
secretary of state.

Wilson was anxious to maintain Polaris as a viable system to counterbalance improved Soviet antiballistic missiles (ABMs). In 1967, he instructed the Atomic Weapons
Research Establishment (AWRE) to commence studies for
the Polaris Improvement Programme (PIP). The full cabinet was not informed.

Wilson decided to go ahead with "Antelope," as the PIP
was known, instead of purchasing Poseidon missiles. The
Heath government proceeded with the PIP, which included
both the Initial Project Definition Phase in 1971 and the

development of a variant of Antelope called Super-Antelope in 1973. Super-Antelope was later renamed the Chevaline Program. Wilson continued this project when he returned to office in 1974. In that year, he told the cabinet about Chevaline (in reality, PIP) although an ad hoc committee of ministers had already decided to continue with tests scheduled for 1974, regardless of what the cabinet might say when they found out about the project.

The Wilson government from 1964 to 1970 maintained other nuclear delivery systems in addition to the Polaris force and continued Labour's intense commitment to NATO. It also maintained a close association with the United States, despite enormous party opposition to U.S. involvement in Vietnam. Despite considerable pressure from President Johnson, Wilson refused to commit even a token British force to Vietnam. This government implemented a major, and much needed, reorganization of defense decision making, notably by carrying out Healey's plan to establish a unified Ministry of Defence. Defense expenditure was decreased, however, and the government was compelled to reduce British commitments east of Suez and in the Mediterranean. Although the Conservatives fervently opposed this program, it was not reversed during the Heath administration. It should also be pointed out that although Labour reduced the defense budget, expenditures were maintained at significantly higher levels than under Margaret Thatcher's Conservative government.

In its last defense White Paper, three months before its June 1970 election defeat, the Wilson government was able to survey its period of office with some satisfaction:

> Britain enters the Seventies with an overall military capability which no other Western European power can surpass. . . . While our military commitments are being reduced . . . the nation is getting better value for the money it spends on defence; thus, despite the reduction in expenditure imposed by our economic needs, we have been able to increase our contribution to the defence of

Europe which is vital to our survival and simultaneously to reduce the over-stretch from which our forces have suffered in the past.[16]

The Wilson-Callaghan governments in the 1970s were subject to even greater pressure to reduce defense expenditures. Britain's economic difficulties, exacerbated by the oil price increases after 1973 and the mismatch of commitments and resources, placed enormous pressures on the defense budget. Party conference and party activists proposed manifesto commitments and conference resolutions calling for reductions in defense expenditures. According to Patrick Seyd:

> The Left held a view of the Soviet Union, distinct from that of the Right, which influenced its view of defence policy requirements. . . . [It argued] that the Soviet Union was a status quo power concerned more with the consolidation of territory than expansion, that military expansion in NATO member-countries would create internal problems for the Soviet leadership and that ideological confrontation, perpetuated by the Soviet leadership, was more concerned with maintaining internal stability within the Soviet bloc than with external aggression. The Left therefore argued that Britain should take a lead in reducing arms expenditure since this would reduce international tensions and would not be exploited by Soviet aggression.[17]

On March 21, 1974, a few weeks after its election victory, the government announced in the House of Commons that it had "initiated a review of current defence commitments and capabilities against the resources that, given the economic prospects of the country, we could afford to devote to defence."[18]

The defense review stressed the government's commitment to NATO; however, it also stated that to achieve its economic, military, and political (tacitly including party political) objectives, Britain's defense forces had to be concentrated in those areas in which they were more effective:

> This meant that NATO—the linch pin of British security—should remain the first and overriding charge on the resources available for defence; that our commitment outside the Alliance should be reduced as far as possible to avoid overstretching our forces; and that general purpose forces should be maintained as an insurance against the unforeseen.[19]

Contributions were to be concentrated in those areas in which the government believed "that Britain can make the most significant contribution to her security and that of the Alliances."[20] Among the commitments to be maintained was

> the NATO nuclear deterrent. NATO strategy is founded on the triad of conventional, tactical nuclear and strategic nuclear weapons. The Polaris force, which Britain will continue to make available to the Alliance, provides a unique European contribution to NATO's strategic nuclear capability out of all proportion to the small fraction of our defence budget which it costs to maintain. We shall maintain its effectiveness. We do not intend to move to a new generation of strategic nuclear weapons. We shall also maintain our tactical nuclear capability, in accordance with NATO strategy.[21]

Successive defense White Papers throughout the remainder of the decade reveal the degree to which the strategy was implemented. The final February 1979 statement on the defense estimates pointed out that despite shrill criticism and acute difficulties and consequences imposed by economic factors,

> [Britain] is the only European country to commit forces to NATO in each of the three elements of the triad on which the Alliance's strategy of deterrence

depends. . . . The United Kingdom continues to concentrate its efforts on those areas where its resources will
most effectively aid collective Allied defence: the defence of the United Kingdom base and its immediate
approaches; the Eastern Atlantic and Channel; the
Central Region of Europe; and the nuclear forces.[22]

By the mid-1970s the Ministry of Defence was thinking
seriously about a successor to Polaris. This caused the Labour government some anxiety because Labour had been
committed in each election manifesto since 1966 not to replace it. Prime Minister Callaghan concluded that no decision needed to be made until 1980. Polaris would remain
serviceable until the 1990s. The government's military advisers approached Callaghan in 1978 and stated that a decision by 1980 was vital. Yet studies had to be undertaken.

In his autobiography *Time and Change*, Callaghan was
eager to point out that his government did not make a
decision to replace Polaris, but

> decided to have a study made by officials of the factors
> that would affect the future of the UK deterrent. The
> terms of reference were strict and limited. The pream-
> ble stated that no decision on the future of the deter-
> rent would be needed during the lifetime of the present
> Parliament, which could conceivably have ended in the
> autumn of 1978, or at the latest 1979. The study
> should examine and report on all the factors which the
> next Government of whatever Party would need to take
> into account in reaching a decision. It was instructed
> not to make recommendations, but to put forward the
> facts and balanced arguments on which cabinet deci-
> sions could be taken. Its sole purpose, said the terms of
> reference, was to provide the basis on which a fully
> informed decision could be taken. Officials were given a
> year in which to complete the study.[23]

In mid-1977, the cabinet revived the prospects for Polaris replacement. The proposal was not revealed to full cabinet or to the Defence and Overseas Policy Committee, but

only to those senior ministers who were reviewing Chevaline. The group was secret and its membership select. It established two committees, one to examine the political and military implications of replacing Polaris, the other to examine potential alternatives. Labour's defeat in 1979 ended the process.

Prime Minister Callaghan's influence on the 1979 general election manifesto was obvious and subject to a great deal of criticism from those whose draft manifesto had been supplanted. Callaghan's version reiterated the importance of détente and arms control negotiations. It emphasized continued reductions in the proportion of the nation's resources devoted to defense, "so that the burden we bear will be brought into line with that carried by our main allies."[24] This is virtually the same phrase used in the February 1974 manifesto. The 1979 document repeated the earlier commitment to renounce "any intention of moving towards the production of a new generation of nuclear weapons or as a successor to the Polaris nuclear force. . . . We reiterate our belief that this is the best course for Britain."[25] The 1979 manifesto did not propose abandoning Polaris or other British systems, however; nor did it criticize the continued presence of U.S. nuclear weapons in Britain or Europe. Thus, this manifesto represents the last in the line of moderate pro–U.S. defense positions.

Labour's Non-Nuclear Defense Policy, 1980–1989

The following summary of Labour's non-nuclear defense policy has been gleaned from a number of sources: the party manifestos of 1983 and 1987; "Defence and Security for Britain" (1984); "The Power to Defend Our Country" (1986); speeches by party leaders and defense and foreign policy spokesmen, and NEC statements. The party documents are not entirely consistent, even where intended to be. They were written between 1980 and 1989 and reflect the thinking of different individuals at various stages of the party's evolving policy.

The Wilson government from 1974 to 1976, and the Callaghan government from 1976 to 1979, wrestled with the problems that have beset most Labour leaders: how to respond to the demands of a party that was largely unsympathetic toward nuclear weapons and was ambivalent toward the United States, the Soviet Union, and the rest of the world, as well as how to balance increasing defense commitments with diminishing resources. Both governments maintained a high degree of continuity with postwar administrations, especially their commitment to NATO and collective security, their concentration of defense resources in Europe and the NATO area, their maintenance of the special relationship with the United States, and their continuation of a British strategic nuclear deterrent. The ground gradually shifted under this long-held stance, however. The 1979 election defeat accelerated the party's rejection of the moderate outlook of the Wilson-Callaghan years, particularly in regard to defense policies.

The 1980 conference was held in the context of a resurgent peace movement, an intense debate on Polaris replacement, and INF deployment. The historical ambivalence felt toward both the United States and the Soviet Union resurfaced in the 1970s and reached its peak in the 1980s. A concept of equilateralism emerged, subscribed to by the European left and many others; the Reagan administration was thought to pose as great a threat to world peace as the Soviet Union. The resolutions passed at the 1980 conference reflected the left's growing domination of the party. From that moment, Labour officially had a non-nuclear defense policy.

This upheaval in the Labour Party coincided with what was perceived by most of the European left as reckless global militarism promoted by the newly elected Reagan administration. U.S. officials offered the idea that a limited nuclear war could be fought (in Europe) to a favorable conclusion. The administration appeared more interested in the deployment track of the INF decision than it was in negotiation. The Strategic Defense Initiative (SDI) program

Reagan advocated was regarded as destabilizing and provocative. In the eyes of Labour activists and others, the intervention in Lebanon, the invasion of Grenada, and the efforts to destabilize the Sandinistas compounded Washington's sins and further justified Labour's defense position.

Besides adopting a non-nuclear defense policy after its 1979 election defeat, the Labour Party moved leftward in all areas of foreign policy, which not surprisingly put them at odds with the Reagan administration. As Bruce George and Tim Lister point out,

> These developments in themselves made it inevitable that Labour would be at odds with the incoming Reagan administration. They were fuelled by a deteriorating international environment which predated the inauguration of President Reagan. There was superpower rivalry in southern Africa, the Horn and in South-east Asia, the Soviet invasion of Afghanistan and Washington's first misgivings about the Sandinistas. In Europe the inept handling of plans to deploy the neutron bomb had undermined confidence in the quality of NATO strategy and the US commitment to Europe, while the Soviet Union was deploying new land-based missiles in Eastern Europe.[26]

In a speech at Harvard's Kennedy School of Government in December of 1986, Neil Kinnock expressed support for NATO, but explained the reservations that he and his supporters had about NATO's policy of nuclear deterrence:

> There is probably no fallacy more dangerous than the view that military strength *alone* is all that is required for security for, as a former Chief of the UK Defence Staff put it, "to pose an unacceptable risk to the enemy automatically poses the same risk to oneself. . . . " That consideration obviously became particularly acute when that military strength is manifested in the form of *nuclear* weapons, when military strategy is dominated by overwhelming dependence on *nuclear* weapons

and when the "unacceptable risk" in Europe is therefore
posed not only by an opponent's possession of weapons
but also — for the first time in history and because of
the very nature of nuclear weapons — from the use of
our own weapons. Against that background I, in common with many others who do not share my politics,
believe that current NATO strategy rests on increasingly untenable assumptions.[27]

Kinnock's speech reflected the Labour Party's desire to for-
mulate a defense policy that did not rely on British nuclear
weapons, but did not completely forsake the concept of
deterrence.

The Labour Party sought to alter NATO's deterrence
strategy, particularly the doctrine of flexible response that
implies a first use of nuclear weapons. In a statement to the
1984 annual conference, the NEC declared:

It is most unrealistic and extremely dangerous to believe that a nuclear war could be limited and controlled.
The danger is that some military strategists believe
otherwise, and that NATO's current strategy of possible "first-use" of nuclear weapons, "controlled escala-
tion" and "flexible response" give credibility to such
delusion.[28]

The party questioned whether the United States would
actually risk Washington for London. Kinnock himself had
stated that he would never press "the button" releasing
British nuclear weapons. Journalists have tried unsuccess-
fully to obtain a similar commitment from him since the
new policies were formulated.

In the 1987 election, Kinnock made it clear that he
would not expect a non-nuclear Britain to be protected by
U.S. nuclear weapons. In an interview with the *Independent*, he said, "The use by America of nuclear weapons will
relate to its interests of defending the United States of
America, and not on other interventions. It's always been a
peculiar sort of umbrella, with damn great holes in it."[29]

Labour's ambivalence toward Polaris persisted. The 1983 manifesto stated that "we will propose that Britain's Polaris force be included in the nuclear disarmament negotiations in which Britain must take part."[30] In 1987, the manifesto stated that "Labour will decommission the obsolescent Polaris system."[31] It was not made clear to the electorate exactly how and when this would be implemented. Kinnock said it would be done almost immediately after he entered Number 10 Downing Street, but others argued that it would be wiser to include it as part of an agreement negotiated with the Soviets.

There was little ambivalence toward the Trident program, which would be canceled. Any money saved would be used "to pay for those improvements for our army, navy, and air force which are vital for the defence of our country and to fulfill our role in NATO."[32] There were those, particularly on the party's left, who were deeply resentful of this commitment to transfer resources to other sections of the defense budget and would have preferred to see them go to the health service, education, or any other socially desirable area of public policy. Some proposed that Labour commit itself to a policy of long-term reductions in defense expenditure, but in the short run, the party should use the money saved by canceling Trident for conventional force expenditures.

Some members of the party began to realize that there might not be any money left at all by the time Labour was elected and began to implement its policies. At the time of writing, most of the money has been spent or is contractually committed.

The party was consistently and fervently opposed to deploying cruise and Pershing missiles. The 1987 party manifesto stated that "success in these efforts to negotiate the removal of all intermediate nuclear missiles in Europe would be warmly welcomed. It would mean the removal of America's Cruise missiles here in Britain and in the rest of Europe, as well as Pershing IIs in Germany."[33] A Labour government would also renounce other nuclear tasks. British forces would give up their nuclear-free-fall and nuclear

depth charges. The BAOR would surrender its five regi-
ments of nuclear artillery and the regiment of Lance sur-
face-to-surface missiles. All British dual-capable systems,
such as the strike-attack squadron of Tornadoes, would be
confined to purely conventional roles.

The presence of U.S. and British nuclear weapons and
bases on British soil and in British waters has also been
controversial. The Labour Party said that it would remove
all these forces, including the submarine base at Holy Loch
(which in any case is to be closed) and insisted that the dual-
capable F–111 aircraft perform only conventional missions.
Although the party recognized the importance of U.S. conventional forces and weapons, it stated that "the current
nuclear roles of some US forces and facilities in Britain are
unacceptable."[34] Some flexibility about timing and consultation emerged, but there was a veto threat about the use of
even conventional facilities.

Labour's goal was to facilitate the establishment of nuclear-free zones in Europe and elsewhere, which, it argued,
would provide an impetus for nuclear disarmament. Only
by setting an example could the party convince Britain's
allies to seriously consider its arguments for decreasing
NATO's dependence on nuclear weapons. British disarmament would be implemented in consultation with the allies,
but the party was resolute in its goals. Labour had often
maintained that some steps would be unilateral and others
multilateral and that "unilateralism and multilateralism
must go hand in hand if either will succeed."[35] In his Fabian
tract *Labour and a World Society*, Denis Healey stated:
"The realities of the problem we face have too often been
confused and distorted by the argument between so-called
unilateralists and multilateralists. The Labour Party has
never believed that it is possible to achieve its objectives by
unilateral action alone, or by multilateral action alone."[36]

Labour was a strong advocate of world disarmament
even before the advent of nuclear weapons. It wished to set
an example to the rest of the world and lead the global movement for nuclear disarmament. Although some were skepti-

cal, many party members felt that independent initiatives by a Labour government might accelerate the process.

Opposition to nuclear weapons was driven by three very different arguments. The first—a deeply felt moral revulsion—had been an important strand in party thinking for decades. The second position, developed for consumption by a largely skeptical public, was that the U.S. nuclear guarantee was no longer credible. Third, the party alighted on the justification of opportunity costs. Money saved by canceling the emerging Trident system would be used to strengthen Britain's and NATO's conventional defenses.

The list below, although far from comprehensive, gives a more complete picture of Labour's defense policies, by indicating what the party opposed as part of the non-nuclear defense policy:

- new conventional strategies such as Follow-On Forces Attack (FOFA), AirLand Battle, and AirLand Battle 2000
- NATO out-of-area operations
- British out-of-area operations
- the British and U.S. forward maritime strategy
- the unconditional sale of weapons abroad
- nuclear proliferation
- the arms race
- battlefield nuclear weapons
- short-range and long-range INF
- overemphasis on emerging techniques
- the development of new space weapons, including antisatellite weapons
- SDI
- the neutron bomb
- chemical and biological weapons

Once the party had committed itself to abandoning British nuclear weapons, it emphasized, to the chagrin of some of its supporters, enhancing its contribution to NATO. The party adopted the concepts of defensive defense and defensive deterrence, about which much has been written. Most, although not all, of these strategies were seen at the time as impractical, but Labour endeavored to provide a degree of detail in their support. In recent years, NATO had emphasized the need to strengthen its conventional forces, which gave a sense of justification to this "modern way" of protecting Britain. Although Labour welcomed the growing importance of conventional weapons and the diminishing reliance on nuclear forces in the alliance strategy, it stated that "we are concerned that these proposals do not go far enough."[37]

Labour's 1982 program, based in part on the work of the NEC Defence Study Group, sought briefly to outline a conventional defense policy. The program stated that the emphasis should be to create military forces recognizably equipped and deployed for defensive purposes: "This will mean maintaining an adequate naval and air defence contribution."[38] Much more thought went into the policy document "Defence and Security for Britain." According to Mike Gapes, head of the international staff at Labour headquarters:

> For the first time the Labour Party conference had set out a comprehensive defence policy statement which attempted to reconcile the strong emotional anti-nuclear arguments . . . with the defence and strategic arguments being put forward with increasing sophistication by academic critics of NATO's existing strategy on both sides of the Atlantic.[39]

The document stated that

> a defence policy is a kind of political signal . . . if Britain acted positively within NATO and deliberately aimed to re-orientate the whole of NATO strategy towards a defensive conventional posture . . . this could have a profound influence on diminishing tension in Europe and improving relations between the blocs.[40]

Labour's belief that British defense policy should be for defensive purposes only was based on the premise that real security comes from the prevention of war.

"Defence and Security for Britain" committed Labour to the defense of the United Kingdom; to NATO, which a British Labour government helped create and sustain; and to collective security in NATO, although it called for major changes in alliance strategy. It stated that Britain and its allies should adopt a non-nuclear defense policy to deter and resist the Soviet Union, on the premise that nuclear weapons were strategically unnecessary and dangerous. It also stated that the party should press NATO to accept a "no-first-use policy" and eventually to eliminate nuclear weapons entirely. Britain's and NATO's conventional forces would be improved, and barriers, obstacles, and other primarily defensive weapons would be deployed.

The aim of the defensive defense strategy was to dissuade a potential enemy from attacking. The theory is that if both states involved in a conflict have defensive defense policies, neither will be able to launch a serious offensive. It follows that if nations can show their interests to be purely defensive, tensions will be reduced and crisis stability increased. The likelihood of a preemptive attack would decrease as well.

This policy would have been difficult to implement, however. It was the opposite of the prevailing NATO strategy of first use and flexible response. It would have had to overcome enormous resistance from many NATO governments and certainly from NATO military strategists. At the time, a nuclear-free zone in Europe would have been difficult to achieve even if NATO were to have eliminated its weapons.

The French nuclear *force de frappe* had a stronger popular basis of support and its dismantling was unlikely. Moreover, if Britain had implemented a defensive defense policy and abandoned its nuclear weapons, France would have become the largest (and only) West European nuclear power, a prospect many outside France found unattractive. The FRG would also probably have objected because the plans for a European defense required it to become the main battleground in a European war.

In outlining the options for a defensive defense policy, Gapes proposed that the Allied Forces Central Europe (AFCENT) be strengthened and that a policy of defense in depth be introduced. Units of light infantry would be deployed along the Central Front, armed with antitank weapons and other precision-guided munitions (PGMs). The most interesting feature of the plan was the defensive use of barriers and fortifications that do not play a part in current NATO strategy. Gapes cited Lawrence Freedman's suggestion that such barriers on the Central Front could reduce the speed of a Warsaw Pact armored advance by one-third and increase its casualties by 60 percent.[41] This concept did not enjoy much support in the FRG.

At that moment, defensive defense had many conceptual shortcomings, as well as military, political, and economic difficulties. Many objections challenge its underlying philosophy and its tactical, strategic, and economic feasibility. From Labour's perspective, the major advantage of defensive defense was that it did not require nuclear weapons. The party also argued that the costs of PGMs would be lower than that of an offensively armed force; a $50,000 missile could be used to destroy a $1 million tank. The concept of defensive defense did not appear in the review of defense policy conducted in 1989.

Labour's reliance on conventional arms placed great emphasis on the BAOR and Royal Air Force (RAF) Germany. "Defence and Security for Britain" stated that "our policy is to change the role of BAOR," which might be reduced in size should the Mutual and Balanced Force Reductions (MBFR) negotiations succeed.[42] A reformed maritime strategy might restructure the RAF to perform more defensive roles rather than its current deep-strike tasks. This restructuring would require a higher investment in radar, in Identification Friend or Foe (IFF) systems, as well as in additional aircraft. Overall, the strategy placed greater reliance on less expensive weapons platforms.

The Labour Party has always had an affection for the Royal Navy, but the navy would have to operate without its current array of nuclear weapons, particularly the nuclear depth bomb (NDB). The non-nuclear defense strategy would be based on an enhanced navy to defend the country's sea supplies, to prevent invasion, and to maintain communications. While in opposition, the Labour Party has made great play of attacking the government's contraction of the surface fleet and pledged in its 1987 manifesto to "maintain a 50-frigate and destroyer navy."[43] The House of Commons Defence Committee report, released in June 1988, provided a great deal of support for those who argued that Britain needed to reverse the decline of the fleet: "We note the steady decline in the number of escorts, and we view with the greatest concern the prospect that the size of the destroyer/frigate fleet will fall below the government's own target of about fifty ships."[44]

The disadvantage of enhancing conventional capability has been the increased cost. Prior to developments in Eastern Europe at the end of 1989, economic constraints suggested that although modest improvements in conventional forces were realistic and desirable, dramatic progress toward any notion of conventional adequacy was nearly impossible. Many socialist parties have had difficulty reconciling their plans for improving conventional defense capabilities with the level of spending they are prepared to support. Some of the policies that seemed to many to be dangerous, wrong-headed, and irrelevant in the 1980s are now perceived in the new strategic environment to be an acceptable part of NATO's agenda.

Arms Control and Disarmament, 1981–1989

Labour has a long-standing desire to "beat swords into plowshares." Before World War I the party bitterly opposed the naval arms race with Germany and advocated working with fellow socialist parties to rid the world of the threat of war. That policy failed dismally. After the traumatic national experience of World War I, the Labour Party, in coalition government and in opposition, sought to create an international environment favorable to peace. In the 1922 manifesto, Labour pronounced that "through the League of Nations an agreement can be reached for a limitation of armaments, with general disarmament as the goal."[45] A year later, disarmament was described as "the only security for all nations."[46]

The development of nuclear weapons, which Labour regarded with repugnance, brought a greater urgency to the peace process. Labour released statement after statement demanding that Britain and the world draw back from the nuclear abyss. Unilateral and some multilateral action by Britain was seen as a step toward creating a nuclear-free world. Paradoxically, there was a coincidence of opinion between Labour's objectives and ex-President Reagan's stated goal of a world free of nuclear weapons; for a while, Reagan was frequently cited as being in support of Labour policies!

Once it had established a non-nuclear defense policy, Labour emphasized the need to halt and reverse the nuclear arms race and regularly criticized U.S. security policies. Two periods of arms control and disarmament policy can be distinguished during the past few years. After the party's non-nuclear defense policy was declared, the attitudes that prevailed changed dramatically with the improvement in East-West relations and the return of arms control to the international agenda in 1987 – the year of the INF agreement and of the progress on the CSCE process in Vienna.

Until this time, Labour and other socialist parties had little success in implementing their non-nuclear defense policies. In its policy paper "Europe: New Detente," published before the 1987 election, the party spoke of its role in creating the new détente. This could not be done in isolation. Labour emphasized the need to breathe new life into the Helsinki process and other arms control initiatives. The 1983 manifesto expressed the following belief:

> We can begin to influence events by the way we present the imperative case for disarmament. In Government we can carry that influence much further by example

and by common action with others. We must use unilateral steps taken by Britain to secure multilateral so-
lutions on the international level. Unilateralism and
multilateralism must go hand in hand if either is to
succeed. It is for this reason that we are against moves
that would disrupt our existing alliances, but are re-
solved on measures to enable Britain to pursue non-
nuclear defence policy.[47]

The NEC issued a statement welcoming Mikhail Gorbachev's February 27, 1987, speech as a constructive step toward ridding Europe of all intermediate-range nuclear missiles. The NEC apparently believed that Gorbachev had
accepted the advice of European socialist parties and no
longer insisted that an INF missile agreement be linked to
the U.S. Star Wars program. Labour had supported a zero-
zero option since it was put forward by Foot and Healey in
1981. It also argued for a narrow interpretation of the Anti-
Ballistic Missile (ABM) Treaty, sought to make the Non-
Proliferation Treaty (NPT) effective, supported the reduction of strategic weapons in START, and advocated a
comprehensive test ban treaty. The party pushed for NATO
to adopt "no first-use" of nuclear weapons and regularly
urged European nations to create nuclear and chemical
weapons–free zones in Europe, the Balkans, the Baltic, Ibe-
ria, and elsewhere. In 1983, Labour repeated its demand for
the removal of all nuclear weapons from Europe and the
surrounding waters. The party also supported the nuclear
freeze movement.

The international situation at the time, particularly
East-West relations, was not conducive to the arms control
proposals of West European socialist parties, however. Ironically, several polls done in the United Kingdom showed
that the Conservative Party's disarmament policies at-
tracted greater electoral support. The superpowers began
talking, and a wealth of initiatives followed the Reykjavik
Summit. Gerald Kaufman, Labour's shadow foreign secretary, greeted the summit ecstatically, calling it "the best

news for humankind for nearly half a century. . . . This decision transforms the history of arms control and the prospects for it."[48] He repeated the claim that Labour had contributed heavily to creating this more favorable environment:

> Labour has led the world in arguing for nuclear weapons reduction. . . . Now, however, nuclear weapons reduction is a policy adopted and about to be implemented by the two nuclear superpowers. The most welcome possible world developments have caught up with what Labour has been advocating for many years. Labour's policy for non-nuclear defence will now plainly be part of a continuing world nuclear disarmament process. The unilateralist nature of our non-nuclear defence policy has been overtaken by other countries doing what in the past we would do alone if necessary. *These developments are therefore an endorsement of Labour's stance.* They also stimulate the conviction that more can and will be done. Labour's wish to proceed in Britain with a non-nuclear defence policy fits sensibly and logically into continuing world nuclear disarmament.[49] (Emphasis added.)

Not everyone attached quite the same significance to Labour's input as Kaufman did.

In March 1988, the NEC approved a draft statement issued by the International Committee entitled "Disarmament in Europe." Although the document was released before the party conference, it was the most recent statement of Labour's disarmament policy at the time. (Obviously, the party would not make significant policy statements before the review process was complete.) The paper reiterated support for the INF and further arms control measures, such as the START talks and a comprehensive test ban treaty, and reaffirmed its goal of a "nuclear-free Europe" and, eventually, a "nuclear-free world." It condemned the Thatcher government for obstructing both the current negotiations and progress toward future accords. It also called for comprehensive negotiations that would include NATO and the Warsaw Pact's conventional and nuclear weapons delivery systems and launchers, that would remove the imbalances of conventional forces on both sides, and that would create conventional stability at the lowest possible level.[50]

Political parties cannot devise policies in a vacuum but are periodically obliged to place them before the electorate. Until 1983, defense and foreign policy rarely figured prominently in elections. This situation was changed, however, by Labour's adoption of a non-nuclear policy and the shattering of the defense consensus. The following chapter will examine the role the party's defense policies played in the important general elections of 1983 and 1987.

3

The General Elections
of 1983 and 1987

The 1983 Election

Labour's non-nuclear defense policy was firmly established
by the 1983 election. Within the party, the center of gravity
had completely shifted away from the center-right Atlanti-
cist wing. In 1981, Michael Foot, a longtime antinuclear
protestor, was elected party leader. The manifesto had a
decidedly unilateralist tone; the only mitigating influence
was provided by the Atlanticist/multilateralist wing,
which, though much reduced by defections to the SDP, did
manage to insert some ambivalence into the manifesto on
the issues of Polaris and multilateralism. The manifesto
was described by election specialist David Butler as "a document full of shaky compromises."[1] A leading shadow cabinet member was alleged to have called it "the longest sui-
cide note in history." As one might expect, the pursuit of
peace and disarmament was central to the document and to
the subsequent general election campaign.

Despite the depressed economy and high unemployment rates, the 1983 election was little short of a disaster
for Labour. Labour won 28 percent of the popular vote, only
2 percent more than the SDP/Liberal Alliance. Defense
played a significant role in the election and in Labour's de-

feat. More people than in any other postwar elections stated that defense was an issue that affected their electoral choice.[2] The polls conducted by Market Opinion Research International (MORI) indicated that the percentage of people mentioning defense as an issue they would consider when voting increased from 15 percent to 29 percent from April 21–25 to June 1–2. Those who mentioned disarmament increased from 16 percent to 25 percent over the same period.

The high percentage of people who rejected Labour's unilateralist stance was a significant stumbling block. A Harris poll found that 74 percent of the public believed that Britain should retain an independent nuclear deterrent. The Conservatives were the party of choice among those who considered defense to be a significant issue; Labour simply did not win votes – and most certainly lost a large number of them – because of its defense policies. The public believed that Labour would not keep Britain "safe."

Labour's difficulty with defense was not merely a result of unpopular policies; it also had to deal with intraparty conflicts that arose from differing interpretations of the manifesto. Michael Foot and Denis Healey contradicted each other several times, particularly on the timing of abandoning Polaris. The manifesto declared that "we will propose that Britain's Polaris force be included in the nuclear disarmament negotiations" and that the Labour government would, "after consultation, carry through in the lifetime of the next Parliament our non-nuclear defence policy."[3] Early in the campaign, Healey said that Polaris would only be decommissioned if the Soviet Union presented adequate concessions. Foot was unable to clarify the situation. Confirming Healey's statement would seem to refute the manifesto, but public disagreement with his deputy leader was also an unsatisfactory response. The issue dominated the media for several days.

On May 25, former Prime Minister James Callaghan made what one author considered "the most notable speech of the election, carefully released to make the maximum

impact."[4] It explicitly renounced a unilateralist defense policy. The speech kept the division within the Labour party in
the headlines and highlighted Labour's internal difficulties
yet again. It is ridiculous to blame Callaghan for the electoral defeat, however. Labour's fate had been sealed long
before.

Despite predictions that memories of victory in the
Falklands War of 1983 would fade and the Conservative
lead would again decline in the opinion polls, Margaret
Thatcher was still riding the crest of a wave of popularity
(42 percent) in May and June 1983. It is difficult to believe
that in December 1981, the Conservatives had only 27 percent of the vote in the opinion polls.[5] The "Falklands factor"
dented Labour's election hopes substantially, primarily because it highlighted the defense and security issue. Many
viewed Labour's unilateralist policies as weak compared
with the perceived strong leadership of Margaret Thatcher.

The 1983 General Election was a disaster for Labour
and since 1945 no outcome had been more widely predicted.
The party's campaign was inept, poorly run, and disorgan-
ized; it continually directed attention to its own weakness-
es, rather than those of the Tories. The campaign suffered
from continuing internal warfare over the collapse of the
Callaghan government, the formation of the SDP, the ac-
tivities of radical left-winger Tony Benn, and its most inap-
propriate party leader, Michael Foot. The party was unable
to capitalize on the lagging economy and the high rates of
unemployment.

Two days after the party's election defeat, Michael Foot
announced he would be resigning as party leader in the
autumn. Foot's choice to succeed him was the then shadow
education secretary Neil Kinnock—who declared his candi-
dacy within hours of Foot's decision. The other candidates
were Roy Hattersley and Peter Shore, both former cabinet
members, and the late Eric Heffer.

Neil Kinnock was elected party leader at the October
1983 party conference with 71 percent of the votes. This
majority gave him the authority he needed to rebuild

the Labour Party, which direly needed to be unified and modernized.

The 1987 Election

Throughout the early part of 1986, the UK's economy continued to worsen with high interest rates, unemployment still above 2.5 million, and a sterling crisis that at one point nearly resulted in parity with the dollar. By September 1986 Kinnock was fairly optimistic about the party's chances at the next general election. The party had been ahead in the opinion polls for eight consecutive months and the Conservative government had been severely shaken by the Westland affair and resignations from the cabinet. Labour's hopes soon disintegrated, however, when the defense issue erupted once again at the October party conference.

Kinnock visited the United States in the hope of convincing the British public that if Labour were elected it would not create a rift in the British relationship with the United States. He gave a speech at the Kennedy School of Government in which he tried to explain his vision of a Labour government's relationship with the United States on the issue of defense.

On December 10, 1986, the party launched its defense campaign as a result of the party conference. The document, "Modern Britain in a Modern World: The Power to Defend Our Country," was meant to be a preemptive strike to negate internal party dissent and Tory misrepresentation. It laid new emphasis on the need to build proper conventional defenses and on the choice between that and reliance upon nuclear weapons. It was clear, however, that the leadership had little faith in the proposals and that because the policy was internally inconsistent and evasive a nonnuclear campaign could not be sustained.

A further danger lay with a second visit to President Reagan, which senior party members felt would only serve to highlight the defense policy even more, especially if

Reagan tried to embarrass Kinnock. On March 27, 1987, Reagan saw Kinnock for less than the half-hour he had been allotted. This was seen by many in the party as one of several attempts to humiliate Kinnock. The leadership returned to the United Kingdom feeling very bitter. Labour also fell to third place in the polls.

Labour's 1987 general election campaign was, on the whole, professional, disciplined, and effective, for which the party gathered unprecedented accolades. Kinnock himself was praised for the energy and verve he put into it.

The party remained more or less united during the campaign. Though Kinnock displayed a single-minded determination to succeed, he did not believe that the party could win the election, aiming to limit the Tory majority to 40 to 60 seats if possible. If Labour could not show that it was the clear challenger to the Tory Party, it was just about finished. Defense again proved an Achilles' heel; the policy Labour presented to the electorate would have been difficult to carry out, and the party was unable to explain to the electorate how it would be implemented. The Conservative policy of maintaining the nuclear deterrent was simple, easily understood, and very successful.

In one sense, Labour's non-nuclear defense policy was doomed from the outset. The majority of the population still favored a nuclear deterrent and feared the Soviet Union's response should Britain unilaterally disarm. In April 1987, a month before the election was announced, 67 percent of people polled, when asked the question, "Do you think Britain should/should not continue to possess nuclear weapons as long as the Soviet Union has them?" responded that they wanted to keep nuclear weapons. In May 1987, 70 percent of the respondents opposed adopting a policy of eliminating nuclear weapons "even if other countries have theirs."

All parties agreed that conventional defense should be maintained and strengthened so that the issue focused on the nuclear aspect of Britain's defense. Labour was compelled to concentrate too much on the nuclear issue, rather than question the government's plan for effective conventional defense or point out the consequences of the Conservatives' defense expenditures. Labour failed to exploit the mismatch of increasing commitments and diminishing resources. The public took no interest.

The quality of debate on defense issues was poor on all sides. Peter Jenkins, an analyst for the *Independent*, said that "the future of nuclear deterrence has been dealt with at the intelligence-insulting level of what do we do if the Russians invade Britain?"[6] Jenkins accused both the Conservatives and the Labour Party of ignoring the superpower relationship, Mrs. Thatcher of being Gaullist, and Mr. Kinnock of spouting "mostly rubbish." He felt that the issue had been discussed at an emotional, rather than rational, level and that the public had been treated as ignorant of and incapable of dealing with a complex issue. The Conservatives, however, successfully translated the question "Should Britain retain its nuclear deterrent?" into "Should Britain continue to defend itself?" A poster campaign was waged depicting a British soldier with his hands held high in surrender and a caption reading "Labour's defence policy." Opponents warned the electorate that a Labour defense policy would leave Britain defenseless, would break up NATO, and damage the special relationship with the United States. Defense was also used as an example of how leftist Labour had become, an implicit threat that a Labour government would turn Britain over to the Communists in Moscow.

Labour had great difficulty countering its opponents' claims, primarily because it was unable to state its own case simply. According to polls, roughly a quarter of the electorate that was well disposed toward Labour was put off by the defense issue. Significantly, 40 percent of Labour supporters believed that nuclear weapons helped to keep the peace in Europe.

Although Kinnock's policies were generally well received, he failed to convince the electorate when it came to defense. A mistake that he made was an attempt to predict Britain's reaction to a Soviet occupation; he talked of making Soviet occupation "untenable," implying that a conventional army could not resist an invasion by a Soviet army that had nuclear weapons. The public could not understand why he wanted a unilateralist policy. Was it because he was a CND supporter or merely because the conference had accepted the policy and Kinnock had to go along with the decision?

There was little evidence of sustained analysis behind the platform's details. The policy appeared underdeveloped and was not well explained. When questioned, Labour spokesmen often gave rambling replies, which only increased the public's confusion, or made political mistakes, such as Healey's comment about Moscow's praying for a Labour victory. The policy lacked vision. It was not placed in the context of an alternative foreign policy in which the cold war relationships did not exist, and it was rarely promoted with enthusiasm.

In the March/April 1988 issue of *New Socialist*, Mike Gapes argued that Labour's defense policy appeared unconvincing because the leadership attempted to de-emphasize the concept of defensive deterrence. It promoted policies consistent with defensive defense but did not place those policies in a conceptual framework. The result was an impression that Labour was not committed to defending the nation. The debates concentrated on how Britain would fight a war, but, according to Gapes, "real security does not come from fighting wars but in preventing war."[7] Gapes believes that if the party had not backed away from the defense policy it presented in "Defence and Security for Britain," it would have had more success convincing the electorate that it had a well-thought-out and effective nonnuclear defense policy.

The poll data generated during and after the 1987 election highlighted the unpopularity of Labour's defense position. When people were asked which party had the best policy on defense, the Conservatives won every poll.

Polls conducted during the election revealed public support for the Conservatives on most issues. A *Times*/MORI survey taken on May 11–13 and May 29–30 revealed that the Conservatives were considered to have the best team to deal with the country's policies. The *Daily Telegraph*/Gallup survey of May 7–11, published in the *Daily Telegraph* on May 14, showed that the British public believed the Conservatives had the best policies on inflation and prices (52 percent to Labour's 18 percent, with the SDP/Liberal Alliance at 10 percent), Britain's defense (51 percent to Labour's 17 percent and the party alliance with 13 percent), industrial disputes (48 percent to Labour's 26 percent and the party alliance with 11 percent), law and order (45 percent to Labour's 20 percent and the party alliance with 12 percent), and the Common Market (42 percent to Labour's 18 percent and the party alliance with 11 percent). Labour had the best policies on education and schools, unemployment, and the National Health Service. The Harris/*Weekend World* TV program poll of Conservative-Labour and Conservative–SDP/Liberal Alliance marginal constituencies found that the Conservatives did well on defense, taxation, law and order, and the economy. Labour did well in health, education, and employment. The SDP/Liberal Alliance was last, even in its own target seats, on every issue except lessening divisions within Britain.

On June 3–4, MORI conducted its fourth and final poll for the *Sunday Times*. It found that only 31 percent of the respondents agreed with the statement, "We don't need nuclear weapons in order to have an effective defence policy." Sixty-two percent disagreed. Between the first and fourth survey, the number of people who agreed fell by 5 percent, while those who disagreed rose by the same amount. When asked the question, "Should Britain get rid of its nuclear weapons even if other countries keep theirs?" only 24 percent agreed, while a staggering 70 percent disagreed. In its poll on June 8–9, Gallup discovered that while 57 percent believed the Conservatives would give Britain an effective defense policy, only 17 percent thought Labour would, and that 54 percent believed the Conservatives had the best defense policy, while only 21 percent chose Labour. In a poll conducted from the end of May to the beginning of June, Gallup found 53 percent of respondents in favor of keeping Trident and only 35 percent opposed. A number of polls showed that more than 20 percent of those who did not vote Labour listed defense as the principal reason.

The party's defeat at the 1987 election was really a defeat without excuses. Clearly, the party had "fallen down" on policy, the voters had rejected the very character of the party, and the party had shown that it was out-of-date and out-of-line with the public's aspirations. Labour's tax policy was believed by many to have been the main reason for Labour's defeat. The size of the Tory majority shocked the Labour party leadership. Colin Hughes and Patrick Wintour have written that

> out of that disappointment, the ensuing self-analysis, and the compelling need to restore purpose and electability to the Labour party, grew the most comprehensive policy review that the party had ever undertaken. Out of it, too, grew a determination to restructure the party's organisation, and unify its restyled campaigning with streamlined policy-making methods.[8]

During the run-up to the election, Kinnock had changed much of the party's policy-making machinery and had beaten the militant left of the party. These moves gave him an extraordinary command over the party. Most people would have considered it unbelievable, however, that within two years Kinnock would have changed the main element of Labour's defense policy from unilateralism to multilateralism.

4

The Policy Review Process, 1987–1989

The third election defeat in a row prompted a complete review of Labour Party policies. MPs backed the need for one, but Kinnock was not sure what he wanted from it. Tom Sawyer, deputy secretary general of the National Union of Public Employees (NUPE) and chairman of Labour's Home Policy Committee of the National Executive, started the process by preparing a paper that he then sent to Kinnock. Sawyer believed that the way that the party reviewed its policies would almost be as important as the policies that were finally adopted. He saw a review as a means of restabilizing a relationship between the party and the electorate and believed that the review itself would symbolize change.[1]

Sawyer's paper, "An Approach to Policymaking," was approved by the NEC on September 14, 1987. It stated that "it would be unnecessary and wrong to launch into public rejections of policy on which we fought the [1987] election simply because we think they were unpopular. Equally, we cannot start a review with a blank sheet."[2] The aim of the review groups should "not be to embark on wholesale revision of policy, but rather to review some of the key themes and issues":

1. How can we make our socialist values relevant to the majority of the population?
2. Where did we fail to get our message across? Can our policies be strengthened and put across more effectively in these areas?
3. How were Labour policies seen by the people we need to win over? What would make them change?
4. What changes—economic and social—should be expected in the next four years? How can we make Labour's program more relevant to Britain in the 1990s?[3]

After the NEC meeting Sawyer said that "some may mistakenly or unfairly portray these proposals as a new revisionism, and an attempt to swing the party away from traditional principles and socialist values. For those, the only true test of radicalism is a deep conservatism in thought and ideas."[4]

The need to examine security policy closely should have been self-evident to the party after three consecutive election defeats and the contribution made by defense to defeat in the last two. It was also obvious that British, NATO, and Soviet security policies were (and still are) changing too rapidly to permit simple updates of existing policies. The INF Treaty, the possibility of a CFE Treaty and of additional arms control measures, and the improved relationship between NATO and the Soviet Union completely altered the context in which defense policy was shaped. The changing relations within NATO, particularly between NATO-Europe and the United States, also made reappraisal imperative.

In the past, the Labour Party has frequently succumbed to the temptation to "fudge" its policy toward nuclear weapons, hoping that the public would neither notice nor care. Traditionally, it has failed to take note of opinion polls, but the three defeats sharpened its interest and converted the party to the doctrine of "winning elections" even if that meant discarding hitherto central policies where necessary. The Labour Party had to construct carefully a policy appropriate to the current situation, mindful that it could not consider British defense policy as exclusively the prerogative of the Labour Party: the electorate, legislature, Western Alliance, and fellow alliance socialist parties would all have to consider the same issues.

The party had, at least theoretically, a vast range of options from which to choose if it decided to change its defense policy. Many of the options open to the party in 1987 would be closed to the party during the following few years because of the passage of time and the constantly changing international environment. These options are discussed in the following section.

Also facing the party were a number of political opponents, both in and outside Parliament, who could be relied upon to contribute to the electorate's suspicion and hostility during any policy review. Although a degree of uncertainty could be tolerated until a new policy was devised and accepted by the conference, any deliberate confusion would be counterproductive and the lack of a clear position a considerable handicap.

Several factors determined whether or not the party changed its stand. Kinnock's commitment to the future security policy was crucial. Despite his overwhelming majority in a leadership vote in 1988, he did have some difficulty controlling the conference, and the review process was not expected to be free from opposition. Within the party itself, there was strong resistance to abandoning the non-nuclear defense policy, which many believed to be practically, ethically, and ideologically sound. Some believed that the electorate could be convinced that non-nuclear policies were superior and that international developments would make those policies more palatable. Others wished to carry on regardless and refused to succumb to the lure of office.

Clearly many in the party would strongly resist any movement away from the status quo. Ken Livingstone, one of the hard left's most prominent figures, warned that there would be a "civil war" in the party if it abandoned unilateralism. Most of the resolutions on defense submitted to the October 1988 conference reaffirmed Labour's commitment to unilateralism, demonstrating that there was a significant segment within the party prepared to resist any attempt to alter defense policy.

The trade unions would play a crucial role in the future of unilateralism, primarily because of the block voting system used at the party conferences. Ron Todd of the Transport General Workers Union or TGWU (the most important union because of the size of its block vote) was traditionally a unilateralist supporter in addition to supporting unilateralist motions at the 1988 and 1989 conferences. He temporarily withheld his support for Kinnock during the 1988 leadership contest to pressure Kinnock to retain the nonnuclear policy.

It was thought possible that to induce the party to swallow a large dose of revisionism, the leadership might offer activists an anti-American and antidefense policy as compensation.

Though party activists accepted the idea of a review at the 1987 conference, it was clear that they sensed a "sellout." Though Sawyer's proposals were voted through on September 28, the support for the review by the party was precarious. This precariousness was demonstrated by the defense debate on October 1, when the party reaffirmed its unilateralism. Denis Healey and right-wing union leaders spoke out in support of changing policy while the unilateralists argued that unilateralism would have the support of the public if only the leadership supported the policy.

The unilateralists wanted to update, but not fundamentally to change the policy. Although the two sides were ready, Kinnock was not going to begin a battle just yet. Few, not even Roy Hattersley, Gerald Kaufman, or Brian Gould, believed that Kinnock would change his mind on defense.

In October 1987 Larry Whitty submitted the final outline of the review to the NEC. It was proposed that at the next conference, in 1988, a "statement on values, objectives and an outline of Labour's policy programme" should be presented.[5] He proposed that the review groups should

- assess the policy issues and opportunities for the 1990s
- assess the relevance and credibility of existing party policy matched against the needs and concerns of groups of voters
- recommend lead themes of political strategy as well as policy areas in which more detailed examination was required.

Each of these points linked the formulation of policy to the chances of selling it to the voting public. Kinnock was accused of "electoralism" after stating at the October conference that the main consideration of the review was what policies were right or wrong for the 1990s. Kinnock's main aim was to defeat the Conservatives at the next election.

This policy review was to be more tightly organized than previous ones, and each review group's membership was selective and managed by the party. The meeting of the NEC in October finalized the formation of seven policy review groups, each with equal representation from the NEC and PLP. Each had two convenors, one from the shadow cabinet and one from the NEC. The seven groups were concerned respectively with the reductive and competitive economy, people at work, economic equality, consumers and the community, democracy for the individual and the community, the physical and social environment, and Britain in the world.

The progress of the review was monitored by a Campaign Management Team comprising Peter Mandelson of the Shadow Communications Agency (SCA), Charles Clarke, Patricia Hewitt, Larry Whitty, and Geoff Bish. The team had little control over the review groups, most of which produced reports twice their allotted lengths.

The initial studies were presented to and approved by the 1988 party conference. They were set out in a document entitled "Social Justice and Economic Efficiency." According to this 1988 NEC report, "the policy review process is in two distinct phases — and the reports themselves represent the completion of only the first of these phases. In the second phase, the groups will move on to more detailed work on policy development."[6] The entire process hinged on the critical 1989 conference.

The Policy Review Group on Britain in the World

The Britain in the World Group was to examine the party's international affairs and defense policy and decide whether some or all of the unpopular policies previously adopted on defense ought not to be abandoned or modified. Its terms of reference included international relations, common security, the European dimension, defense policy, and the North-South issues of cooperation and development.

Its membership was probably the most carefully chosen of the seven groups, consisting of representatives of the NEC, the parliamentary spokesmen on defense, foreign affairs, and overseas development, plus one member of the European Parliament. During the review the group's joint convenors were Gerald Kaufman, shadow foreign secretary, and Tony Clarke, a trade unionist and NEC member. Kaufman, however, would dominate the group.

Two distinct subgroupings within the group could be identified. The supporters of change included Kaufman, Denzil Davies, shadow defense secretary (replaced by Martin O'Neill), Gwyneth Dunwoody of the NEC, George Robertson, European spokesman, and Tony Clarke of the executive's International Committee. The group opposing change included Joan Lester, a lifelong unilateralist, Stuart Holland, founding member of European Nuclear Disarmament or END, and Ron Todd, unilateralist general secretary of the TGWU.

The Britain in the World Group was serviced by the NEC's Policy Directorate, especially Mike Gapes and Kaufman's assistant, Matthew Hooberman. The bulk of the work began after the group's visit to Moscow in February 1989. The draft report was then transmitted to the other committees of the NEC and submitted for approval by the NEC in May 1989. Prior to being submitted to the party conference in October 1989, the entire document, including the defense and foreign affairs proposals, was published and circulated to the CLPs and the trade unions. The unions' votes were to be crucial.

Kaufman and his colleagues sought a successful formula, one that would create a manifesto that would appeal to the electorate and avert civil war within the party. The aim was to create a consensus, but not by obfuscation. A clear position and a popular policy had to be produced that would satisfy the party, the public, and the views of the NATO allies. Kinnock had spoken ad infinitum about the need to update the policies, particularly to meet "the challenges and opportunities of the 1990s."[7] Critics saw this as a move to the right — an attempt to capture the lost middle ground of British politics. Changes proposed by Kaufman would be debated at the 1989 conference, which would not necessarily accept the recommendations of Kinnock, the Policy Committee, or the NEC. Ron Todd warned that the conference, not the leader, would decide Labour policy.

The group decided not to deal with defense issues during the first year of the review, but Kaufman and O'Neill did tour European capitals to sound out the new thinking on defense issues. The reasons for the delay were that the START talks were under way; a NATO decision was imminent on modernizing short-range forces in West Germany; Gorbachev's disarmament proposals were announced; and a Democrat might be elected to the White House.[8]

Kaufman was daunted by the task ahead of him and his group. He regarded it as the "biggest responsibility of his career, because it was the only one on which, in his eyes, the whole future of the Labour party depended." His aim was "to construct a policy that was clear, internally consistent (and therefore credible), and electorally saleable."[9] he decided to confine himself to pure policy and to let Kinnock's office cope with delivering it to the party and the people.

The reactions of the trade unions to new proposals at the conference were seen as the deciding factor. At that time, the unions fell roughly into two groups. Foremost

among those supporting the unilateralist line were Todd's
TGWU; the National Graphical Association (NGA); the
National Union of Railwaymen (NUR); and the Manufac-
turing, Science and Finance Union (MSF). The Society of
Graphical and Allied Trades (SOGAT) and the Fire Bri-
gades Union (FBU) also fell into this category.

The second group of unions was in favor of nuclear
weapons and included the Amalgamated Engineering
Workers Union (AEWU) and the Electrical, Electronic, and
Plumbing Trade Union (EEPTU). The leaders of both these
unions had a very high profile because of their opposition to
the party's defense policy since the mid-1980s. It was hoped
that a majority of these unions would be amenable to the
leadership's persuasive powers.

The likelihood of a dramatic change in defense policy
also depended upon the recommendations that the Policy
Review Committee would make and upon its perception of
the options available to the party. It was felt that if anyone
could succeed in uniting seemingly irreconcilable view-
points it was Kaufman, but even his intellect and political
acumen faced a formidable challenge.

Labour's Options in 1987

Nuclear options available to the policy review team in 1987
ranged from the pure unilateralism of 1983 to the fudged
unilateralism of 1987 to replicating the elements of the Conservative government's nuclear policy—a four-boat Trident
flotilla, a variety of substrategic nuclear forces, free-fall nuclear bombs, nuclear depth charges, and U.S. Lance missiles. As pointed out earlier, the team was to reject any form
of unilateralism. Several party members and analysts rede-
fined unilateralism to include some bilateral and multilateral steps, but these despairing efforts failed.

A number of options centered on keeping the Trident but canceling the fourth boat—SSBN-08 (HMS Vener-
able). There was a precedent for this in the cancellation of

the fifth Polaris submarine by the incoming Labour government of 1964. Although the Royal Navy would dislike losing its fourth Trident, it would just about be a viable force. Barring accidents, the Royal Navy could still maintain its commitment to have one boat permanently on station. This option could placate some in the party who might still resent the abandonment of unilateralism, but the viability of a three-boat option would need to be convincing politically and strategically to justify canceling a submarine on which more than £120 million had already been spent.

Kinnock's Role in the Review

Kinnock had achieved three crucial changes after the 1987 defeat that resulted in the publication of the policy review's work. First he "drove a wedge" between the Campaign Group and the soft-left at the top of the party, a move that created an alliance between the right and the soft-left of the party on the NEC and that gave Kinnock unprecedented authority. Second, he created joint policy committees that ended the distrust that had damaged relations between the shadow cabinet and the NEC over the past ten years. In turn, the joint committees created the cooperative structure needed for a successful two-year policy review. Third, in 1986, Kinnock had set up the Shadow Communications Agency manned by marketing and communications experts and headed by Peter Mandelson and Philip Gould. The SCA gave the Labour Party a professional look, and a new corporate identity was designed to demonstrate that Labour was an innovative party shedding old associations and images. These three developments helped make the policy review a political success.

The Conservatives were to claim that the U-turn on unilateralism was for electoral convenience and questioned whether Kinnock had genuinely changed his mind. The turning point for Kinnock, however, had been the superpower summit in Iceland in October 1986. He was convinced that the superpowers were now serious about nuclear disarmament, a fact that created opportunities that would have appeared unthinkable merely two years previously. Although certain that British nuclear weapons could be negotiated away in return for Soviet cuts, he could not risk damaging the party by declaring that unilateralism was finished. It was also too late to make changes to the election manifesto. Unilateralism was deeply embedded in the constituencies and the trade unions and was almost an untouchable part of the defense policy. Nor was there a multilateralist movement within the party, except among some shadow cabinet members. Kinnock could only edge the party in the "required" direction.

In December 1986 the party leaders had presented a defense campaign document designed to show that Britain must choose between conventional or nuclear weapons. Kinnock and Healey realized that proposing to abandon Trident was inadequate. Unilateralism and membership of NATO were inconsistent. Nearer to the election, Kinnock and Healey moved away from airtight unilateralism, emphasized the consequences of the commitment to NATO, and stated that the party would allow the United States to continue operating their facilities in the United Kingdom. This policy had proven a mess. After the election, Mike Gapes summed up Labour's problem on nuclear weapons and defense policy in general:

> The sad fact is that on defense issues most people are not willing to listen to rational arguments. Research indicates that most people would rather not think or talk about these issues at all. When pressed to do so, they fall back on crude stereotypes and emotional responses. Einstein said that nuclear weapons had changed everything except the way people think. It appears that in Britain, at least, little has changed in the last 40 years in this respect. As long as British people see nuclear weapons as a kind of national status

symbol then it will be extremely difficult to introduce a coherent and rational defense policy to this country.[10]

Martin O'Neill, the deputy defense spokesman, believed that no one took Labour's defense policy seriously. He realized that Gorbachev was a new kind of Soviet leader, that the INF talks were near completion, and that the Trident program was too advanced to be stopped. Other front benchers were also changing their views, but, of course, they would make little impact unless Kinnock also changed.

Yet shortly after the 1987 defeat there were no public signs that he would change. "In private, however, Kinnock was much more convinced that the policy had to be altered. Both the electoral imperative, and the possibilities for disarmament in the nineties, required change."[11] He was not to demand change through a single speech, however, because it would have preempted the policy review process. "Whenever change came, Kinnock wanted to ensure that it would be permanent; he would not waste energy on a battle that he felt unconfident of winning."[12] Though Kinnock in his television interviews at the 1987 conference offered hope to those of the shadow cabinet who wanted change, Kaufman and O'Neill were still unsure what Kinnock thought.

The Interim Report

As noted earlier, the Policy Review Committee released an interim report that was approved by the NEC in May 1988. It was condemned by the Campaign Group as revisionist — a movement away from traditional values. Four-and-a-half paragraphs were devoted to defense, which repeated some often used phrases (e.g., "Labour will also work to achieve the mutual dissolution of NATO and the Warsaw Pact"). It also expressed moral revulsion toward nuclear weapons, which "create hostility and distrust which stunt the lives of individuals and communities across the world."[13] More important was what the report *did not* say about defense. One paragraph states that "Labour welcomes the INF Treaty and the quickening pace in arms reduction negotiations between the superpowers. A strategic arms reduction treaty will have little impact on the Trident program."[14] The treaty released the party from its commitment to remove such weapons from British soil, a move that would have damaged NATO. It also now appears that cuts in the U.S. budget and arms control agreements will lead to reductions in the U.S. conventional presence in Europe.

The interim report made no specific reference to Trident, to decommissioning Polaris, or to U.S. nuclear bases. The section on defense acknowledged the rapidly changing international situation and the importance of awaiting the outcome of negotiations. It was apparent that the Britain in the World Group, the NEC, and the parliamentary leadership preferred to keep their collective heads down and their options open. This, however, fueled the arguments of those who sensed a sellout.

The Evolution of the Trident Issue

By the time of the next general election Trident will no longer be merely a concept. Three of the four submarines are already under construction, and the order for the fourth was expected later in 1991. The first submarine, HMS *Vanguard*, will enter service in the mid-1990s with the remaining submarines following at yearly intervals.

As of March 1991, the estimated cost of the Trident program is £9,863 million (at an exchange rate of £1 = $1.56). SSBN-05 (HMS *Vanguard*) is 77 percent completed, SSBN-06 (HMS *Victorious*) about 59 percent completed, and SSBN-07 (HMS *Vengeance*) about 39 percent completed; £120 million has been spent on SSBN-08 (HMS *Venerable*).[15]

By the end of 1991 nearly 6 billion of the £9.8 billion will have been spent, and most of the rest will be contractually committed. Built-in cancellation costs also made it difficult to scrap the project once under way. Each submarine contract includes a break-clause to compensate the builders, Vickers Shipbuilding and Engineering, Ltd. (VSEL), in case of cancellation. The break-clause for HMS *Vanguard* was 125 percent of the contract value, and all subsequent clauses were 100 percent of the contract value.

Kinnock recognized that by 1991–1992 Polaris would be reaching obsolescence, and it would be possible to cancel only the fourth Trident submarine. His politics were evolving with "ups and downs," from the naive unilateralism he once expressed.

Improved East-West relations and arms control also added to the uncertainty of Trident's future. Some believed the United States might cancel the Trident D-5 as part of a future arms control agreement. Where would such a decision leave the United Kingdom? The House of Commons Defence Select Committee reported in 1987–1988 that "the Prime Minister has sought and received assurances from the United States that the supply of Trident missiles to the UK will in no way be affected by any future arms control agreement."[16]

Since the 1987 election defeat, with the submarines moving closer to deployment, many in the party, both inside and outside Parliament, became more openly critical of the non-nuclear defense policy and its attendant unilateralism. Peter Shore, a former Labour cabinet minister, wrote that "unilateral nuclear disarmament has done great and demonstrable damage to the Labour party; it is a policy that is, at least, irrelevant to the search for peace and disarmament and should be dropped at the first opportunity."[17] He called for Labour to rethink its defense policy:

> Looking ahead, if we retain our existing policies they will look even more absurd. We will still be members of NATO, and NATO strategy will still be indivisible. . . . It would be simply folly for Britain to unilaterally abandon its new Trident fleet, and it would be equally foolish for us to negotiate it away on a bilateral, one-for-one, basis with the Soviet Union. The arithme-

tic is obvious. If Britain possesses 500 Trident warheads and the Soviet Union 6000, what on earth could we gain by eliminating our 500 and leaving the Russians with 5,500 to threaten us at will?[18]

Some signs of flexibility in defense thinking began to appear in Kinnock's speeches at the 1987 and 1988 party conferences and in some interviews he gave. On "This Week, Next Week," the TV program broadcast on June 5, 1988, Kinnock was asked, "You were a unilateralist CND supporter. Was that appropriate to the time and not so appropriate now?" He replied:

It was very appropriate at the time because absolutely nothing was happening. Or rather, more correctly, what was happening was a perpetual build up and in those circumstances the effort to try and break the logjam was very important. The logjam is broken — the President of the USA and the General Secretary of the Communist Party of the Soviet Union walked together in Red Square and both said their objective is to rid the planet of nuclear weapons and. . . . have actually practically started to go about the business. It isn't just a matter of sending pleasant messages to each other, it's actually getting on with it. Now in those circumstances, what we have to consider is how best to accelerate the process towards greater security and diminish dependence upon these aggressions and antagonisms that have been in existence throughout both our life times.[19]

Later Kinnock was asked whether he wanted to eliminate the Trident system now, to which he replied:

No, the fact is no, but it doesn't have to be something for nothing. The fact is now that it can be something for something. Now, I say that now, even before the first paragraph of the strategic arms reduction treaty has been drawn up and the reason I say it is because it is already clear that bilateral reciprocal missile for missile reductions between any part of the West and the Soviet Union has been on for some time. . . . There is something for something, there can raise a reduction in nuclear arms as a consequence of the initiative we are prepared to take.[20]

This answer appeared to indicate that unilateralism, like John Cleese's famous parrot, was dead, defunct, deceased, expired. Kinnock even hinted that a Labour government would accept NATO's possession of nuclear weapons under the U.S. nuclear umbrella: "The United States of America will have nuclear weapons for as long as the Soviet Union has nuclear weapons and vice versa. I also understand, as everybody should, that NATO is a nuclear alliance and that we shall continue to be part of NATO."[21]

The television interview in which he indicated that he had abandoned unilateralism created a furor, as a result of which Kinnock was compelled to "clarify" his views in a newspaper interview. According to Peter Jenkins's article in the *Independent*, November 16, 1987, "In the first interview that he has given since the loss of the general election . . . [Kinnock] gave a strong indication that he is moving away from unilateral nuclear disarmament towards a multilateralist approach."[22] In the interview with Jenkins, Kinnock returned to his position before the television interview.

Then, in a paper presented to the North Atlantic Assembly (NAA) Study Group, "NATO in the 1990s," Martin O'Neill, as a junior defense spokesman (now shadow defense secretary), hinted that the party was reconsidering its stand on Trident. On December 15, 1987, the *Times* commented, "A Labour defence spokesman moved his party a step further away from unilateralism by calling for Trident to be included in the East-West disarmament talks.[23]

Composites 55 and 56

Those supporting a change in defense policy made the first overt move at the 1988 party conference. A motion proposing multilateral, bilateral, and unilateral means of reducing Britain's nuclear defenses was drawn up by Mike Gapes for

Charles Clarke. Tony Clarke of the Union of Communication Workers (UCW) would then submit the motion, but his union voted to make the text more unilateral. The General and Municipal Boilermakers Union (GMBU) added an amendment reinserting "multilateral." At the 1988 conference, these union-tabled ideas became Composite 55, supported by Kinnock and the leadership, which upset the unilateralists. The resolution reaffirmed "its commitment to the total elimination of all nuclear weapons in the world to be brought about by steps of unilateral, bilateral, and multilateral nuclear disarmament." It supported the INF Treaty and further arms control negotiations and condemned the Conservative government for purchasing Trident and its "obstructionist and isolationist stance, regardless of the progress being made towards nuclear disarmament by international effort."

Composite 55 was invoked by the UCW and introduced by Alan Tuffin, their general secretary:

> This motion is not a fudge, neither is it a soft option and neither is it a backing away . . . but we are fed up with the arguments about "isms." Unilateralism, bilateralism, and multilateralism are often put forward by people arguing their point as if they are diametrically opposing strategies. In fact, they are all important.[24]

The resolution was supported by John Edmonds, general secretary of the GMBU, who said that there was little point in making an isolated gesture when it was possible to create large-scale reductions in the global nuclear arsenal: "We have to plan step-by-step the achievement of a nonnuclear Britain that will make the world safer."[25]

The unilateralists saw the motion as a tactical maneuver, and CND began to pressure the delegates. Composite 55 was opposed by the TGWU and several smaller unions. The vote was closer than most had anticipated; the TGWU's 1.25 million votes and the 203,000 votes controlled by the three smaller unions that voted against the resolution at the last minute were all that stood between the leadership and success.

Several unilateralist resolutions were presented to the conference. Composite 56, for example, called for a campaign for the unilateral removal of all nuclear weapons and bases from the United Kingdom. The leadership opposed the motion, which was carried by 3.75 million to 2.471 million votes. It was supported by the TGWU, which played its usual vital role at the conference with its 1.25 million block vote (one-twelfth of the total conference vote).

The defeat of Composite 55 and the passage of Composite 56 were not seen as indications that the leadership would be unable to change policy. The Composite was really a holding position until the review could be completed. Although Kinnock was disappointed, it was clearly possible to muster a majority for a changed policy next time and reverse the majority on the unilateralist vote in the future. It would only need two medium-sized unions or a larger union to change its allegiance to reverse the results. Unilateralism could be defeated at the 1989 conference. The review group continued to explore a wide variety of options, and Kaufman said that the defeat would not "straitjacket" his review. Kinnock stated, "It is our duty to secure a policy for defence and nuclear disarmament that can secure the support of the people of our country. This is what we will continue to work on. The votes were not conclusive. The policy review goes on."[26]

Challenges over Leadership and Policy

The *Observer* (October 2, 1988) reported that Todd of the TGWU was determined that the "policy review on defence is not to be allowed to succeed unless it reaches his union's chosen conclusion."

During 1988 Kinnock's leadership was challenged by Tony Benn, and the more vulnerable position of his deputy leader, Roy Hattersley, was challenged by Benn's running mate, veteran left-winger the late Eric Heffer, and by the soft-left John Prescott. Benn and Heffer ran a "Campaign for Socialism" that included the following proposal: "Britain should be working more actively for peace throughout the world, by diverting arms expenditure to the needs of development; by adopting nonalignment, outside of all military blocs and without foreign bases on our soil."[27] Benn and Heffer tabled a motion that demanded a £7 billion reduction in defense spending and a ban on British participation in any nuclear programs. The leadership challenge mounted a two-pronged attack—opposing changes to Labour's current policies and objecting to Kinnock's style of leadership, which the far-left and some of the right denounced as authoritarian. Defense entered the debate as a result of Kinnock's attempts to move away from unilateralism.

The conference overwhelmingly reelected Kinnock and Hattersley. In addition, Kinnock's position was reinforced at the beginning of the 1988–1989 session of Parliament when the PLP elected a largely supportive shadow cabinet. This was interpreted as an affirmation of Kinnock's modernizing approach. Not one of the 21 members elected could have been construed as being hard-left; six belonged to the center-right and 15 to the soft-left. The prominent frontbench spokesmen who would play an important role in formulating and interpreting policy were clearly pro-Kinnock and promodernization and represented the majority of the party. The October 1988 party conference thus completed phase one of the review.

Yet a report published in August 1988 by the Institute for European Defence and Strategic Studies called "MPs and Defence" indicated that there was still strong support for unilateralism. A survey of 171 MPs, including 55 Labour, indicated that 45 Labour respondents were opposed to an independent nuclear deterrent. Only 16 percent of the Labour sample saw the Soviet Union as the main threat to world peace. These figures could have overstated the support for unilateralism because some respondents may have been cautious about revealing their opposition to such a fundamental plank in the party's platform.

A most important display of the new thinking was a Fabian pamphlet called "Working for Common Security" that appeared in January 1989 and provided the first clear case for multilateralism that the party had ever had. It was given considerable publicity by the national papers.

The Work of the Review Group

Kaufman's group began the bulk of their work after their visit to Moscow, Washington, and several other world capitals early in 1989. During the arrangements for the review group's Moscow visit, Kaufman was told that his group would be able to meet senior Soviet officials. Kaufman had to decide whom to take to Moscow. Though Kaufman eventually decided on a four-man team, his decision to take Todd was particularly difficult. Todd could be an "unguided missile," but if he were converted during the visit, a unanimous report could be delivered to the party. In addition, having a unilateralist in the group would add credibility. Kaufman decided to take Todd, who accepted, also accepting Kaufman's condition that Kaufman alone would be spokesman during the trip. To the press's annoyance, Todd did not make a wrong move during the whole trip.

Kaufman dropped unilateralism after the Soviets told him during the visit that they wanted all five nuclear weapons states to negotiate away all nuclear weapons by the year 2000. The Soviets also did not want bilateral negotiations, which O'Neill had long opposed, because they did not wish to split NATO security into more than one center of decision making. Thus, after the Moscow visit both the bilateral and unilateral approaches were dropped.

Kaufman began work on the review before visiting Washington because he had all the answers he needed from the Soviet Union.

> He wanted to cast the policy as part of a process, with an argument moving forward to its logical conclusion about the future of long-range weapons, including Tri-

dent. He would judge it a failure if the thesis could be
seen simply as a way of getting the party out of an
electoral problem; it had to be intellectually persuasive
too.[28]

Five hours later the draft was complete and was altered
little between then and its acceptance by the NEC in May
1989. Kaufman left a copy with Kinnock before going to
Washington. The March visit to Washington demonstrated
to Kaufman that the Bush administration was serious
about arms control after START I. The administration told
Kaufman that Britain's independent deterrent could be put
into future START talks. On April 8, Kaufman went to see
Kinnock, prepared to resign if Kinnock rejected the paper.
Other than asking for minor changes, however, Kinnock
liked the work. The party leadership believed that it would
be possible to devise a policy that would satisfy Britain's
security needs, the requirements of NATO strategy, and the
party's previous commitment to a non-nuclear defense.

As the two-year policy review drew to a close in April
1989, the nine-strong review team met three times to discuss the draft. There was a danger of a split in Kaufman's
group when the soft-left minority of the group demanded
the adoption of a policy that involved nuclear weapons being negotiated away within the lifetime of a parliament. The
plan *did not*, however, tie the party to an *absolute commitment* to abandon nuclear weapons during the lifetime of a
Labour government. Kinnock had recently made it clear
that he expected the party to abandon unilateralism and to
adopt multilateral negotiations to achieve a non-nuclear objective. The first draft of the group's new defense policy
document did not refer to a time scale. The group's unilateralist members (Stuart Holland, Joan Lester) were prepared
to accept a negotiated approach but also sought a compromise formula that would be acceptable to the unilateralists
in the movement. The issue of a time scale was the only one
on which the group voted. Though Lester and Holland were
in the minority, Kaufman and O'Neill allowed an amendment stating Labour's support for eliminating nuclear

weapons by the year 2000. No one in the group argued against dropping the requirement that the United States remove nuclear weapons from its British bases. Without this agreement, the group might not have been able to present a unanimous report to the NEC. Todd was ill or involved with the dock strike and sent a proxy who took no part in the discussions. Copies of the document were delivered to members of the NEC on the Saturday before the NEC meeting.

The seven policy documents were submitted to the NEC policy "summit" meeting held at Transport House on May 8 and 9, 1989. Because the leadership was determined to drop unilateralism and adopt a multilateralist approach to nuclear arms reductions, defense was the most controversial element to be voted on by the 31-member NEC.

The leadership hoped that the results of the policy review on defense would form the basis of its challenge at the next general election and that the review would herald a "new" and "modern" Labour Party; unilateralism had cost the party two general elections, and it would affect the party's efforts to modernize and to be electable. Kinnock still saw nuclear weapons as immoral and still wanted to get rid of them, but the party's senior members felt that improving superpower relations and arms control gave the party the chance to capture the public spirit and to move along with the changes. Kinnock's opponents would be ready to accuse him of naked political expediency, yet his decision to abandon his lifelong support for unilateralism was one of the most critical and difficult political decisions he has had to make. The defense document set no timetable for the removal of nuclear weapons, nor did it mention unilateralism or multilateralism as ways of achieving disarmament.

The Fight over the New Policy

Kinnock did run into difficulties, however. Ron Todd submitted a paper to the NEC meeting that expressed his strong dissent from the policy document. The Labour left was furious that the document assumed that a Labour government would be committed to NATO – that is, would drop unilateralism – and that only one Trident submarine would be canceled, with the rest (and Polaris) being bargained away in arms control talks with the Soviet Union. Both Labour left-wingers and the Conservative Party made a mockery of the policy of not being the first to use nuclear weapons. The Labour left prepared a campaign to keep the commitment to unilateralism. There was the possibility that the shift on defense could provoke sharp differences in the executive and severe internal opposition in the run-up to the conference in October 1989 and that some front-bench spokesmen could resign over the issue.

Kinnock was confident that the NEC would "rubber stamp" the dropping of unilateralism, and he staked his authority on winning the backing of the party as a whole. If the NEC did back him, he could sweep aside left-wing opposition, but several members of the NEC would likely press for a time scale on the removal of nuclear weapons.

At the meeting Kinnock passionately denounced unilateralism, using the bluntest language yet:

> I have gone to the White House, the Kremlin and the Elysée and argued down the line for unilateral nuclear disarmament. They were totally uncomprehending that we should want to get rid of nuclear missile systems without getting elimination of nuclear weapons on other sides too. . . .
>
> I am not again going to make that tactical argument for the unilateral, independent abandonment of nuclear weapons without getting anything in return. I will not do it.[29]

When the vote came Tuesday, May 9, the NEC voted 17 to 8 to adopt a multilateral policy in which British nuclear weapons would be negotiated with the Soviet Union. Only Tony Benn, David Blunkett, Dennis Skinner, Margaret Beckett, Jo Richardson, Tom Sawyer, Eddie Haigh, and Hana Sell voted against. Clare Short abstained. The NEC did make changes to the defense document. The unilateral-

ists were angered that they had not been offered any concessions. They had tried to get the NEC to adopt the objective
of removing nuclear weapons during a parliament. Kinnock
had defeated Blunkett's attempt to insert a deadline. Robin
Cook's amendment allowing a Labour government to conduct independent bilateral arms talks with the Soviet
Union if superpower negotiations were foundering was
passed without a vote, and the NEC also adopted an
amendment stating that British nuclear weapons were not
a deterrent and were of no practical use.

Ken Livingstone, for the left wing, said, "We intend to
fight throughout this summer to save the party we love and
all believe in." Blunkett vowed to reverse the decision at the
1989 party conference. Then Prime Minister Margaret
Thatcher called the defense policy "unilateralism in a different wrapper," and then defense secretary George Younger
said that it was "about as effective as a feather duster."
Kaufman stated that "the Labour party is now firmly committed through this [NEC] decision to working to remove
British nuclear weapons only by negotiation with other
countries."[30]

Kinnock had achieved a crucial victory repudiating unilateralism, and the NEC vote gave him the chance of winning the backing of the conference in October. One shadow
cabinet member revealed that "Neil has been bursting to
make that speech for two years."[31] Andrew Grice noted that
Kinnock and his supporters were more relieved than
triumphant:

> Labour, they knew, had emerged with a new style poli-
> cy; it would be a watershed in the party's history,
> heralded by the spontaneous applause that had greeted
> the end of Kinnock's speech to the executive.[32]

Kinnock himself said, "We've now got good policies, but
we've got two years of hard selling to convince the public."[33]
Kinnock's greater challenge was to convince the unions and
various unilateralist groupings of the sense of the up-to-

date defense policies. Fifty Labour MPs challenged Kinnock's new position in a letter to the *Guardian* newspaper: "We reject nuclear deterrence. We believe that nations which possess nuclear weapons, if deterrence is to be credible, must be willing to use their nuclear weapons."[34] Most of these MPs belonged to the left wing of the party, including Tony Benn, Ken Livingstone, Diane Abbott, and Bernie Grant.

Throughout the summer, individual trade unions would hold their annual conferences at which they would vote on the new policy review. This was a critical time for Neil Kinnock, as he was able to judge the popularity of the new policy among a section of the party constituting 90 percent of the vote at the party conference.

Those unions opposing the new defense policy were the TGWU, FBU, MSF, NUR, the Associated Society of Locomotive Engineers and Firemen (ASLEF), and the bakers' union. At the TGWU conference the members voted 472 to 367 against the new defense policy. The union would therefore support the motion at the party conference calling for the removal of nuclear weapons within a Labour government's five-year term of office. The union also passed a motion to enter multilateral talks and to disarm unilaterally.

Kinnock spoke at the TGWU conference *after* the unilateral and multilateral resolution was passed. Kinnock's speech "laid it on the line" to the union. He supported multilateralism and said that the delegates were out of touch with the mood elsewhere in the party and the country. "If you set a deadline and say that whatever happens it will be met, there will be no negotiations [with the Soviet Union]," he said. Todd did privately accept after the NUPE vote that the 1989 conference would back Kinnock. He promised not to undermine the new strategy should the party conference accept it.

During August, Labour activists prepared to protest at the October conference over the leadership's plans to push through the new policy without the opportunity for amendments. Constituencies gave notice of their opposition to the dropping of unilateralism. CND even circulated "model" motions to constituencies—many of the motions submitted to the conference were based upon them—calling for the unconditional removal of nuclear weapons within the lifetime of a Labour government. The new policy did, however, have grass-roots support.

In September the Trades Union Congress (TUC) voted by a 7 to 1 majority to support the General Council's statement of a non-nuclear defense policy by multilateral negotiation. A composite motion was moved by the MSF and the National Communications Union (NCU), both committed to unilateral disarmament: "Congress . . . seeks a positive response to recent disarmament initiatives by demanding multilateral and bilateral involvement by Britain and calls on the government to implement unilateral initiatives as speedily as possible."[35]

The Amalgamated Engineering Union (AEU) and the TGWU opposed the motion; the TGWU because it lacked a time limit and the AEU because it included unilateral nuclear disarmament. SOGAT and ASLEF also voted against it. Young of the NCU said that the motion had two motives—to pressure the government to respond to Gorbachev's proposals and to unite the trade unions and the Labour movement. The defense debate had been held late in the day, took less than half an hour, and ended without contributions from any unilateralists. The vote further confirmed the likelihood that the conference in October would approve the new policy.

In October the party conference voted for the new defense policy, although it did carry an NCU motion supporting the policy review statement on multilateral nuclear disarmament, with the objective of a nuclear-free world by the year 2000. The vote on the NCU motion was 3,597,000 to 2,414,000, a majority of 1,182,000 votes. Kinnock's authority enabled him to ignore the vote. This debate did not generate much excitement.

Bruce Kent, former chairman of CND, proposed a motion on defense cuts of £5 billion to the European NATO average, which was carried by a majority of 2 : 1. A hard-line unilateralist motion was defeated by 3,635,000 to 2,431,000 votes.

The motion on defense cuts demonstrated that there was still a deep division within the party. Supporters of unilateralism cheered when Bruce Kent, Todd, and Benn spoke at the debate, accusing the Labour leaders of an "unprincipled" U-turn in an attempt to win an election. Bill Jordan of the AEU was jeered when he said that the new defense policy brought Labour into line with the views of the people it represented.

Kinnock was delighted by the victory of the defense statement but angered by the left's victory on defense cuts and by Joan Ruddock's attack on his attitude toward nuclear weapons. Pat Arrowsmith, vice-president of CND, resigned from the Labour Party in protest. Surprisingly, Todd said that he *would not* campaign to overturn the decision — his union block vote had not been large enough to defeat the support for the policy review. Phase two of the policy review was completed by the 1989 party conference.

5

A New Defense Policy for Britain

The details of the defense policy were published in the new policy document *Meet the Challenge, Make the Change*, made publicly available at the end of May 1989. Clearly a great deal of research, analysis, and intelligence had been put into the review process by Gerald Kaufman and his colleagues. The timing of the review made it possible to take account of changing attitudes and positions in the relationship between East and West and the related changes within the Soviet Union and its leadership. The section on defense was positive, realistic, and forward looking in scope and content.

It opened by stating that the defense of the United Kingdom is a prime responsibility of any government and that the Labour Party has always accepted and acted upon that responsibility. It continued:

> Labour is determined that in the 1990s and beyond Britain shall be properly defended. Defence policy for these coming years must be considered in a context very different from those of the 1930s and 1940s and the decades since. The most bellicose former Cold War warriors proclaim that the Cold War is over, that the Soviet Union is no longer "an evil empire" and that the

challenge today is very different from what it was five years ago, before Mikhail Gorbachev took over the leadership of the Soviet Union.[1]

The document went on to criticize the Conservative government's nuclear and foreign policies and to explain how necessary it is for a defense policy to change as the world situation changes:

> Our overriding charge against the Tories is that they regard weapons and especially nuclear weapons as an end in themselves. Their foreign policy is often reactionary and negative; within its context they tend to treat defence as a discrete issue, separate from and all too often influenced by other highly relevant issues. Clausewitz said that, "war is nothing more than the continuation of politics by other means." So, too, is peace. Defence cannot logically, usefully or constructively be considered except in the context of other world developments.[2]

The "developments" the party saw as important influences upon defense policy include the political changes in the Soviet Union and similar developments in Warsaw Pact states, the economic crises faced by the Soviet Union and the Warsaw Pact because of the defense burden, and the demonstration that nuclear radiation "knows no frontiers" as a result of the Chernobyl disaster. The United States also faced huge twin budget deficits because of the largest arms program in history, so that both the superpowers have very strong economic pressures for peace and disarmament. Finally, the superpowers are now rapidly improving relations, a process started by Reagan and Gorbachev and shown by the INF accord.

The Labour Party recognized that Britain also had to face up to financial constraints on its defense policy, arguing that cost effectiveness should take priority over increasing the defense budget. A Labour government would ensure that the armed forces were efficiently and effectively trained and equipped to deal with challenges to Britain other than those that might arise as a result of being a NATO member. A well-trained, mobile land, sea, and air force is needed, capable of dealing with problems affecting British dependencies outside Europe. A Labour government would also make British forces available to the United Nations Security Council and the Commonwealth for peacekeeping and peace-making duties.

Second, Britain has to be able to anticipate and respond to any threat to itself. A defense policy needs to be able to protect the United Kingdom and provide for the appropriate contribution to NATO, which is significant, from all the armed forces. One specific criticism of the Conservatives' "distorted defense policy" is the lack of provision of new ships for the Royal Navy, which a Labour government would provide "within budgetary constraints."

Thus, there was a strong commitment to the defense of Britain and support of NATO. The party also maintained its hope that the time may come when NATO and the Warsaw Pact are no longer needed for the security of East and West:

> As long as NATO continues in existence the Labour party, pledged and committed to membership of the Alliance, will ensure the continuance of the contribution. . . . We look forward to the time when suspicion and tension between East and West will be sufficiently dispelled for both NATO and the Warsaw Pact to be simultaneously dissolved.[3]

The party saw improved security from the end of the superpower hostilities of the past and from the resulting arms reductions, including the end of the need for NATO:

> For, ultimately, the best defence of Britain lies not in armaments—though as long as they are required a Labour government will ensure that armaments are properly provided—but an end to the mutual distrust and hostility that have bedevilled both East and West since the end of the Second World War. Disarmament, prop-

erly negotiated, properly verified, is becoming an increasingly key element in the defence of Britain and the common security of the world.[4]

A Labour government would commit itself to the process of world disarmament and be determined to play an active and constructive part in that process. The document gave credit to the two superpowers for the progress they had achieved in this area and criticized the Conservative government as being the lone obstructor of the measures of disarmament. The party would not put the country at risk by such a process and argued that it can in fact reduce the threat to the nation's security. "We believe in vigilance wherever it is required. We believe, too, in defending our country through measures to reduce any potential external threat, and disarmament here offers increasing and encouraging prospects."[5]

Labour would seek to eliminate land-based nuclear weapons from Europe because it wanted to reduce the dangers of nuclear war, which nuclear weapons represent, and to eliminate all nuclear weapons by the year 2000. To achieve these ends, the Labour Party supported "fully verifiable international agreements, achieved by negotiation with and between nuclear armed powers," and Labour would take independent steps to "contribute to the process of achieving such international agreements."[6] Encouraging progress has already been made in the INF Treaty, START, in which the present government does not wish to participate, and the removal from the United Kingdom of cruise missiles that the prime minister originally said were needed for Western defense. Previous verification difficulties have also been largely overcome in the last few years, and a Labour government would contribute toward the verification process.

If the party were to win the next general election, it recognized that joining the START talks at such a late stage could complicate and delay the conclusion of the talks, although Labour considers it vital that the United

Kingdom should participate in international nuclear disarmament negotiations at the earliest possible moment.

Labour believed it reflected majority opinion in the United Kingdom and was opposed to Trident from the start. The purchase of the Trident weapon system is seen by Labour as unjustified in defense policy terms for the following reasons:

• It is not "independent"—the missiles are serviced in the United States.

• The missiles are rotated with replacements from the stockpile in the United States.

• The British nuclear capability is not a deterrent. If the Soviet Union were not deterred by the U.S. capability, it would not be deterred by the United Kingdom's.

• No rational circumstance for Britain's use of nuclear weapons would exist when NATO was unwilling to do the same.

• It is being purchased regardless of international agreements over and above NATO's existing nuclear armaments. It invites proliferation, which other governments are working to prevent.

The only role for British nuclear weapons in the new international climate is to further the process of international nuclear and conventional disarmament.

If Labour had won the 1987 general election, it would have been able to cancel Trident, which it saw as wasteful, unnecessary, and provocative. Because of the rate of construction, however, three of the submarines will be under way, so that there will be no financial savings by stopping their construction. Because of the inbuilt penalty clauses, more public money would be wasted canceling than completing the first three. If an order for the fourth submarine had not been placed, it would be canceled by a Labour government and alternative work found for the shipyard, in the form of a hunter-killer submarine that would add to Britain's naval capability in NATO. A Labour government would also cancel Tory plans to increase the number of warheads on Trident compared with Polaris and would also cancel the planned nuclear stand-off missile for the Tornado aircraft.

Thus, upon taking office, a Labour government would adopt a policy of "no-first-use" of British nuclear weapons; encourage the second stage of START between the other nuclear powers; and place all of Britain's nuclear capability, including Polaris and Trident, into international nuclear disarmament negotiations. Polaris and Trident could be included in START II, or, if necessary, Labour would negotiate directly with the Soviet Union and/or others to eliminate that capacity by negotiated and verifiable agreements. Testing of all nuclear devices would also end. If there were no nuclear disarmament talks at the time, Labour would have unilaterally removed British nuclear weapons. "Labour played a signal role in triggering-off the process whereby nuclear disarmament has become a policy actively pursued by the superpowers. Labour should now become part of that process and use the opportunity to the full."[7]

Therefore, to eliminate nuclear weapons by the year 2000, a future Labour government would have initiated a series of steps.

Acting on its own on matters entirely within Britain's individual power of decision, a Labour government would

- adopt a policy of no-first-use of British nuclear capability until Britain is entirely rid of that capability
- end testing of British nuclear devices
- cancel the fourth Trident submarine
- cancel Tory plans to increase the number of nuclear warheads on missiles possessed by Britain
- not proceed with a nuclear stand-off missile for Tornado.

Acting within NATO, a Labour government would

- strongly oppose the modernization of short-range and tactical nuclear weapons within the alliance
- oppose deployment of short-range and tactical nuclear weapons, should a decision to modernize have been taken before Labour comes to office

• seek to secure a widening of the NATO negotiating mandate at the disarmament talks in Vienna to include aircraft and short-range and tactical nuclear weapons
• work for the abandonment of flexible response as a NATO policy
• press for our NATO partners to adopt a policy of no-first-use of any and all nuclear weapons in the NATO arsenal
• take active steps to make the Third Zero a NATO objective.

Acting with the United States and the Soviet Union, a Labour government would

• secure participation in the disarmament negotiations
• place all of Britain's nuclear capability into such negotiations with the intention of eliminating it in concert with action taken by the superpowers.

Acting in the United Nations, a Labour government would

• strongly support an early verifiable agreement on a Comprehensive Nuclear Test Ban Treaty
• insist at all times on a strict interpretation of the Anti-ballistic Missile Treaty
• work for full implementation and strengthening of the Nuclear Non-Proliferation Treaty.

The key point, despite the earlier long list of criticisms, is that a Labour government would not become a non-nuclear power for as long as other nations retain their nuclear forces.

Labour's Defense Policy since the 1989 Vote

Since the publication of the policy review documents in 1989, several important developments have taken place, not least among them the change in Eastern Europe and the reduced Soviet threat.

In May 1990, the NEC approved a 20,000-word, 51-page campaign document, *Looking to the Future*, that summarized the findings of the three-year policy review. Only Dennis Skinner and Tony Benn opposed it. Kinnock said that the document would "further extend our appeal and further strengthen the party," denying that it sold out to socialism.[8] The new document, *Looking to the Future*, is based upon the previous year's publication, *Meet the Challenge, Make the Change*, which completed the second year of the review.

The document was conceived in January 1989 before *Meet the Challenge, Make the Change* was completed. At that point, the party was receiving different results from opinion polls, and the team overseeing the policy review was not certain how the public or the party would take to the review. It had also been feared that there would be a backlash at the 1989 party conference and that motions contradicting the policy review statements might be passed. Thus, it was proposed that the NEC and shadow cabinet draw up a campaign document that would reconcile the motions and the policy review statements. Though the policy review progressed fairly smoothly through the 1989 conference, the plan to produce a campaign document was now dropped. Instead, it was decided that a third phase of the policy review should be created.

Looking to the Future was launched with the promise that the party was in touch with Britain's desire for new policies for a new decade. In the introduction, Kinnock stated:

> We have focussed on the main policy areas and taken account of further changes in Britain, across Europe and in the rest of the world. In doing so, we are responding to a desire from every part of Britain for a new approach to a new decade, we are leading the efforts for change, and we are establishing an agenda for government.[9]

At the NEC meeting the only close vote on the document came from the soft-left, led by Robin Cook and David
Blunkett, and the hard-left, who tried to weaken the commitment to NATO by changing the terminology from the
"need for NATO in the foreseeable future" to "the immediate
future," a change that was defeated 14 to 10. The document
states:

> Labour's defence policy has been entirely vindicated by
> the events of the last year. It will be a firm foundation
> for the new initiatives required by the transformed map
> of Europe.
>
>   Many of the objectives we set out in our defence
> policy have already been achieved or are close to
> achievement. We opposed modernisation of land-based
> short-range nuclear weapons and supported the "Third
> Zero" — in other words, the negotiated destruction of
> these weapons. Within NATO, only Mrs. Thatcher's
> government supports modernisation. Now that Presi-
> dent Bush has announced that modernisation will not
> take place, the Third Zero is implicitly accepted
> throughout the Alliance.[10]

The document adds that recent events make possible
"reductions in United Kingdom defence spending far beyond
anything envisaged at last year's Labour party conference."[11]
    Although acknowledging that there are still some haz-
ards with regard to the Soviet Union, the document states
that now that there is "no realistic threat of invasion from
the East," NATO's doctrine of flexible response has col-
lapsed and that the role of NATO "must therefore be fundamentally reassessed."[12] But NATO will still be needed "for
the foreseeable future" because

(1) we in the West need an organisation to negotiate,
    implement and verify disarmament agreements.
(2) NATO's existence makes it unnecessary for the EC
    to have any military role.[13]

One new element of the document was the section on arms conversion. In early 1990 the Britain in the World Group split into four groups, one covering arms conversion. Martin O'Neill and the TGWU worked together on this issue, preparing plans for an arms conversion agency to help prepare the defense industry for the decline in defense spending. According to the document,

> Labour is determined to make sure that the diversification process happens as smoothly and effectively as possible. . . . diversification offers a tremendous opportunity to strengthen and modernise Britain's civil manufacturing base [and] Labour will ensure that resources made available by the reductions in military spending will be used for restructuring our manufacturing base.[14]

A Defence Diversification Agency (DDA) would be set up to offer technical and marketing advice and other help to companies seeking public contracts because "it is essential to maintain and use the considerable skills and expertise of people working in the defence industry, either by transferring them into civil industry or continuing to employ them in defence companies."[15] The DDA would also provide a fund to supplement the private resources devoted to diversification and would encourage new investment in civil work. In addition, the party also expects the defense industry to develop its own plans for diversification.

The 1990 party conference overwhelmingly endorsed the "Britain in the World" section of *Looking to the Future*. Opening the defense and foreign affairs debate, shadow foreign secretary Gerald Kaufman restated that "Labour's agenda has become the international agenda. The international agenda is Labour's agenda." He believed this was the case because the policies that Labour had been advocating since the early 1980s had now been adopted by NATO or had gained the support of the U.S. administration — such policies

as the inclusion of aircraft in the CFE negotiations and subsequent treaty and proposed negotiations with the Warsaw
Pact to eliminate short-range nuclear weapons. Additional
policies proposed abandoning NATO's policy of flexible response, adopting a policy of no-first-use of nuclear weapons,
and holding a second round of CFE negotiations.

Despite strong opposition from party leadership, the
1990 conference carried Composite Motion 60. This motion
argued that defense expenditures under the next Labour
government be reduced to the average level of other West
European countries and that any savings be transferred to
social and economic programs—the National Health Service, for example, and programs covering pensions, hous-
ing, and education. Although the motion carried, Neil Kinnock made it clear that it would not be part of the election
manifesto.

In January 1991, Neil Kinnock set out the party's strategy for international security in the 1990s in a speech to the
Royal United Services Institute in London. His remarks to
the largely defense community audience went as follows:

> There are and certainly will be diversions from the di-
> rection of change. The course of change may well be
> tragic and it is certainly not going to be smooth. But
> certainly "there is no going back for anyone."
> That, and the accompanying instability, being so—
> what do we in the Labour Party think should be the
> main features of our strategy for international security?
> First, it is going to have to be careful. Not because
> the customary threat to security continues. As Alan
> Clark [a junior Defence Minister] and many others say,
> it doesn't. The care must be taken because the Soviet
> Union is an unstable giant, not because it is a stable
> monolith. . . .
> Second, our international security strategy is for
> negotiated nuclear and non-nuclear disarmament.
> CFE1 was obviously very welcome, we hope that the
> START Treaty will be signed next month and subse-

quently ratified and naturally, we want both to be fully and honestly operated and properly verified. . . .

Third, in our approach to the East-West dimension of international relations, the Labour Party believes that we must use the CSCE process to strengthen the new democracies in East and Central Europe. . . .

Fourth, and closely related to that need to foster democratic strength, the prosperous mixed economies of the West and the Pacific must do more to stimulate and sustain economic improvement throughout Eastern Europe.[16]

He also explained the party's position toward NATO. For years Labour had argued for the mutual dissolution of NATO and the Warsaw Pact. Kinnock, however, made it clear that this was no longer the case:

Meanwhile it appears to me that the interests of both Europe and the United States are best served by NATO to avoid introversion in either continent. That's surely best done by retaining reduced but significant U.S. links with European security. And since NATO will for some time to come be:
 • an important component in the evolution of CSCE,
 • a necessary instrument for negotiation, implementation and verification of disarmament agreements,
 • and a defence alliance,
news of its obsolescence is somewhat exaggerated.[17]

This speech was one of the strongest endorsements of NATO made by a senior Labour politician in at least a decade.

Labour and the U.S. Administration

Also Labour's relations with the U.S. administration appear to have improved considerably. Kinnock visited President

Bush on July 17, 1990 to build upon the improved relationship. In recent months the U.S. ambassador to the UK has talked with Kinnock and the shadow cabinet about Labour's election prospects and the party's rise in the opinion polls. U.S. representatives have also talked to Larry Whitty, the general secretary, and the backbench foreign affairs committee. Although the White House said that it was normal for the president to meet opposition parties, Kinnock said, "I think the political situation in Britain and the strong prospect of a Labour government will not have escaped the President's notice. Everyone else in the world seems to have noticed it."[18] High-level contacts between Labour and the Bush administration have increased since Bush took office because "the Bush administration did not come in with (the Reagan administration's) negative ideological baggage about Labour."[19] Although Bush said that the good relations between Britain and the United States would continue with a Labour government, he said that he did not think Mrs. Thatcher was on her way out just because of the opinion poll results.

During Easter 1990, John Smith led a highly successful trip to the United States to allay fears about the Labour Party. The fact that his visit took place at all is a strong contrast to Kinnock's highly unsuccessful visits to Washington before the 1987 general election.

The leading article of the *Independent* (London) for April 18, 1990 said that "almost certainly the President's comments owe more to the perception that the Labour party no longer represents a unilateralist threat to American bases in this country and that it no longer intends to leave the European Community." Clearly Washington is reassured now. Even David Owen of the SDP praised the policy review in general and also suggested that he might be able to endorse SDP members' return to Labour. He mentioned the possibility of a pact at the next election and perhaps would rejoin the party himself at some stage, although he did not expect the Labour Party to want him.

The Labour Party, the Gulf War, and Beyond

As discussed earlier, the change in Labour's defense and security policy was illustrated by Labour's approach to the Gulf War. Throughout August and September 1990, the party leadership supported sanctions, the naval blockade, and the sending of troops to Saudi Arabia.

On August 30, 1990, Neil Kinnock wrote to then Prime Minister Margaret Thatcher, requesting that Parliament be recalled from recess to discuss the Gulf crisis. Winding up the emergency debate for Labour on September 7, Gerald Kaufman, the shadow foreign secretary, said:

> Why has the world reacted so unprecedentedly to Iraq's invasion and illegal annexation of Kuwait? Some say that the response is simply a self-interested western reaction motivated by concern for oil prices and for oil supplies. I respond to those who offer that argument with a question. Why did Saddam Hussein invade Kuwait? It was not for some noble ideal and it was not even because of his grievance about the adequacy of Iraq's outlet to the Gulf. Saddam Hussein committed his aggression precisely and solely for oil – its production level and its price.
>
> . . . The founders of the United Nations constructed a system that would work only if the five permanent members were in agreement. For 45 years, the cold war prevented such agreement; now it can be and has been achieved, and there is the possibility of a new era in international relations in which the United Nations can work as it was always meant to work. Now, when we demonstrate to Saddam Hussein that the United Nations will not allow aggression to pay, not only will it send Saddam Hussein back out of Kuwait, but it will tell anyone else in any other part of the world who wants to try the same game that they will meet the same fate.[20]

The 1990 Labour Party conference overwhelmingly endorsed the stance taken by the party leadership on the conflict. The NEC statement to conference was carried almost unanimously.[21] The statement supported the sanctions and naval blockade being used against Iraq, but it also made it clear that if these failed, force should be used to free Kuwait. An emergency resolution on the crisis was moved by the Fire Brigades Union:

> Conference therefore calls on the British government to make a clear and unequivocal statement that it will not commit British forces to offensive military operations against Iraq unless they have explicit authorisation through a resolution passed by the Security Council, under the provision of the United Nations charter, which deals with the use of force by the United Nations, and unless it is under its military command.[22]

On the recommendation of the NEC, the motion was defeated by 4,863,000 to 625,000 votes. The Gulf debate was thus a watershed for the Labour Party and for its evolving defense and security policy; conferences of the recent past would have been unlikely to have passed an NEC statement supporting military action, let alone overwhelmingly.

Despite the many differences of the Labour Party and Conservative government on domestic issues, the remarkable cross-party consensus continued throughout the remainder of 1990 and into 1991. Speaking in the House of Commons on January 17, 1991, Neil Kinnock gave Labour's "complete support" to the government and to the British troops now engaged in action.

The emergency debate in the House of Commons on January 21, 1991, also showed the extent of cross-party consensus on the crisis. With the Labour and Conservative front benches accepting each other's amendments for debate, a very substantive motion supporting coalition troops was formulated, calling for the implementation of the UN mandate. Winding up the debate for Labour, Gerald Kaufman said that he did "not have any reservations about going into the same division lobby as the government."[23]

There were of course dissenting voices in the party that did not support the stance taken by the leadership over the conflict. They argued that it was wrong to use force to liberate Kuwait and that the aims of the UN should be achieved by sanctions. These were in the minority, however, as can be seen from the size of the defeat of the emergency resolution at the party conference. The number of dissenting voices within the PLP also declined throughout the conflict as can be seen by the size of the majorities in the House of Commons and the votes within the PLP itself. A motion proposed by two of the dissenting MPs to the PLP meeting on February 20, 1991, was defeated by a 4 to 1 majority. It called for

> a cessation of offensive action to enable a major new round of diplomatic initiatives aimed at securing a negotiated settlement which includes the withdrawal of all Iraqi forces from Kuwait and the calling of a peace conference with the objective of settling all outstanding disputes and achieving international peace and security in the area.[24]

Gavin Strang, the Edinburgh East MP and another critic of the war, believed the Gulf conflict would damage the prospects of the new world order so often mentioned by President Bush. In *The Scotsman*, February 16, 1991, he wrote:

> A war even a few weeks long will still be bloody by historical standards. Some will argue the deaths will be tragic but necessary price, but will the outcome universally be regarded as a victory for collective international action?
>
> For some, it will mean one permanent Security Council member succeeded in pushing through the authorisation for an early war, orchestrated its commencement and provided an overwhelming proportion of the forces aligned against Iraq as well as being in supreme command. . . .
>
> The allied forces should be withdrawn and replaced by UN forces drawn predominantly from the region

and under clear UN control. The UN should expedite a
Middle East peace conference with the objective of set-
tling all outstanding disputes and achieving security in
the area. If, in this way, the UN can show its integrity as
the instrument of justice, the world may yet put faith in
it.[25]

By the end of the conflict, the party dissenters had been
marginalized and in some ways discredited, because they
had all argued that the war would produce thousands of
allied casualties. At the same time, Kinnock had consolidated his standing, both within the party and with the
electorate.

In the *New Statesman and Society* of March 1991, Pro-
fessor Fred Halliday of the London School of Economics
asserted that the stance taken by the political left was a
major blunder and that the only people who should have an
input at a peace conference were those who had supported
the use of force against Iraq.[26]

Obtaining the support of the 1990 party conference for
a multilateral nuclear defense policy was a very significant
event for Kinnock and the party leadership. It indicates
that when the NEC and shadow cabinet meet to draw up
the election manifesto, the party will have a series of pro-
gressive defense and security policies for the 1990s.

Kinnock's and the NEC's position was strengthened further by two events in June and July 1991. First, during the
debate on the Royal Navy in the House of Commons on
June 27, 1991, Martin O'Neill, the shadow defense secretary, stated that Labour may not cancel the fourth Trident
submarine if an order had been placed when the party assumed office. In reply to an intervention from Scottish Na-
tionalist member Dick Douglas, he stated:

> Until such time as an order is in place, no one can talk
> about construction. If an order were placed before a
> general election, an incoming Labour Government
> would have to examine the contract, the cancellation
> charges, and so on. The position on that is clear. It has
> been reported repeatedly that we have said that in the

event of a general election being called after an order has been placed, a responsible Labour Government would examine the contract before cancelling.[27]

Second, a commitment was given by Gerald Kaufman that a Labour government would retain the British independent nuclear deterrent until disarmament negotiations end with an agreement by all nuclear weapon states to eliminate their entire nuclear arsenals. Writing in the *Guardian* on July 10, 1991, he stated:

> To Labour it makes sense for Britain to play a continuing constructive role right the way through the international nuclear disarmament negotiations. We believe that Britain ought to remain as a participant in those negotiations until they are successfully concluded with an agreement by all thermo-nuclear powers completely to eliminate those weapons.[28]

Kaufman's comments were designed to rebut attacks by the Conservative government that Labour would allow Britain to negotiate Trident away, but still leave the Soviet Union with a sizable nuclear arsenal capable of destroying Britain.

The failed Soviet coup and the dramatic arms reductions gave the opportunity for critics to reverse Labour's new defense policy at the October 1991 party conference. A motion calling for the cancellation of Trident was defeated by a two-thirds majority. Although a motion calling for reductions in defense expenditure was passed by a two-thirds majority, the party leadership made it clear once again that it would not form part of the election manifesto.

The Labour Party has dumped a defense policy that contributed so heavily to its loss in the general elections of 1983 and 1987; it has thereby gained its strongest electoral position in many years. Labour now has a set of defense and security policies that need not be feared by the United States, NATO, and, most important for political purposes, the British electorate.

Notes

Chapter 1

1. Malcolm Chalmers, Paul Rodgers, and Malcolm Dando, "Trident Options," *New Socialist*, October/November 1988.

2. House of Commons, *Official Report* 183, no. 36 (January 17, 1991).

3. M. R. Gordon, *Conflict and Consensus in Labour's Foreign Policy 1914–1965* (Stanford, Calif.: Stanford University Press, 1969), 1. According to Gordon, traditional British foreign policy consists of these basic elements: (1) maintenance of a European balance of power, (2) the colonial empire, (3) supremacy of the sea, (4) flexibility and self-restraint, and (5) use of force if necessary.

4. E. Windrich, *British Labour's Foreign Policy* (Stanford, Calif.: Stanford University Press, 1952), 3.

5. *Labour Leader*, February 3, 1911, p. 74.

6. Gordon, *Conflict and Consensus*.

7. 1918 Labour Party Manifesto.

8. 1922 Labour Party Manifesto.

9. 1959 Labour Party Manifesto.

10. David Caute, *The Left in Europe* (London: Weidenfeld & Nicolson, 1966), chap. 14.

11. James Callaghan, *Time and Change* (London: Collins, 1987), 295.

12. 1922 Labour Party Manifesto.

13. Patrick Seyd, *The Rise and Fall of the Labour Left* (London: Macmillan Education, Ltd., 1987).

14. "A Socialist Foreign Policy," 1981, p. 1.

15. Peter Byrd, *Socialist Democracy and Defence: The British Labour Party* (London: British Atlantic Publications, 1984), 1.

16. Fred W. S. Craig, *Conservative and Labour Party Conference Decisions 1945–1981* (Chichester, West Sussex: Parliamentary Research Services, 1982), 134.

17. Ibid., 138–139.

18. Ibid., 139–140.

19. Composite 55, Labor Party NEC report 1988.

20. Composite 56, Labor Party NEC report 1988.

21. Robert Harris, *Observer*, October 9, 1988.

22. See Mary Kaldor, Dan Smith, and Steve Vines, eds., *Democratic Socialism and the Cost of Defence* (London: Croom Helm, 1979).

23. See Robert Trelford McKenzie, *British Political Parties* (Maxton statement on p. 19) and Samuel Beer, *Modern British Politics* (various editions) for discussion of leadership in the Labour Party.

24. Crossman, as quoted by Mark Jenkins, *Bevanism: Labour's High Tide* (London: Spokesman, 1979), 66. Jenkins provides a complete account of the postwar Labour left's history.

25. Craig, *Conservative and Labour Party Conference Decisions*, 147.

26. Byrd, *Socialist Democracy*, 6.

27. Ibid.

28. For a more complete account of international socialist organizations, see Bruce George and Tim Lister, "European Democratic Socialist Parties and NATO," Occasional Paper, Atlantic Council of the United States, March 1987.

29. *Common Security*, report of the Independent Commission on Disarmament and Security Issues (London: Pan-World Affairs, 1982), IX.

30. *Defence without the Bomb*, report of the Alternative Defence Commission (New York: International Publications Service, 1983), 1.

Chapter 2

1. Kenneth Harris, *Attlee* (London: Weidenfeld & Nicolson, 1982), 277.

2. Ibid.

3. Ibid.

4. Ibid., 278.

5. Colin McInnes, *Trident* (London: Brassey's Defence Publishers, 1986), 32.

6. Harris, *Attlee*, 288.

7. Ibid.

8. Ibid.

9. Peter Hennessy, *Cabinet* (Oxford: Basil Blackwell, 1986), 136.

10. John P. Mackintosh, *The British Cabinet*, 3rd ed. (Oxford: Basil Blackwell, 1977), 459.

11. As quoted by Harris, *Attlee*, 291.

12. Hennessy, *Cabinet*, 136.

13. 1955 Labour Party Manifesto.

14. Ibid.

15. Harold Wilson, *The Labour Government 1964–1970: A Personal Record* (London: Weidenfeld & Nicolson & Michael Joseph, 1971), 40.

16. Ministry of Defence, *Defence White Paper 1970* (London: HMSO), 1.

17. Seyd, *The Rise and Fall of the Labour Left*, 31.

18. House of Commons Debates (Hansard), March 21, 1974.

19. Ministry of Defence, *Defence Review 1974* (London: HMSO), paragraph 17.

20. Ibid.

21. Ibid.

22. Statement of Defence Estimates, February 1979, paragraph 132.

23. Callaghan, *Time and Change*, 553.

24. 1979 Labour Party Manifesto.

25. Ibid.

26. Neil Kinnock, "Components of Security: Defence, Democracy and Development," speech at the Kennedy School of Government, Boston, December 2, 1986.

27. Bruce George and Tim Lister, "Labour and Mr. Reagan: A World Apart," *Small Wars and Insurgencies*, April 1990.

28. "Defence and Security for Britain," statement to Annual Conference 1984 by the National Executive Committee (Labour Party, 1984), 8.

29. Anthony Bevins, "Kinnock Reaffirms Non-Nuclear Policy," *Independent*, June 21, 1988, p. 1.

30. 1983 Labour Party Manifesto.

31. 1987 Labour Party Manifesto.

32. Ibid.

33. Ibid.

34. "Defence and Security for Britain," 22.

35. 1983 Labour Party Manifesto.

36. Denis Healey, *Labour and a World Society* (London: Fabian Society, 1985), 7.

37. "Defence and Security for Britain," 26. For a useful discussion of Labour and new technology, see D. Kechane, "New Weapons Technology and the Defence Policy of the British Labour Party," in Ian Bellany, Tim Huxley, eds., *New Conventional Weapons and Western Defence* (Oxford: Cass, 1987).

38. *Labour's Programme 1982*, 240.

39. Mike Gapes, "The Making of Labour's Defence Policy," *New Socialist*, March/April 1988, p. 41.

40. "Defence and Security for Britain," 22.

41. Gordon Burt, *Alternative Defence Policy* (London: Croom Helm, 1988).

42. "Defence and Security for Britain," 29.

43. 1987 Labour Party Manifesto.

44. Defence Committee Report, "The Future Size and Role of the Royal Navy's Surface Fleet," June 1988.

45. 1922 Labour Party Manifesto.

46. 1923 Labour Party Manifesto.

47. "Europe: New Detente," Labour Party policy paper, 1987.

48. Statement of Gerald Kaufman, November 27, 1987.

49. Ibid.

50. "Disarmament in Europe," Labour Party draft statement, March 1988.

Chapter 3

1. David Butler and Dennis Kavanaugh, *The British General Election of 1983* (London: Macmillan, 1985).

2. All polling data published monthly in the *Guardian* (Gallup) and the *Daily Telegraph* (MORI) and compiled by Steven Wise of the House of Commons Library. The authors are solely responsible for the interpretation of the data.

3. 1983 Labour Party Manifesto.

4. Butler and Kavanaugh, *The British General Election of 1983*, 96.

5. See note 3, this chapter.

6. Peter Jenkins, *Independent*, June 10, 1987.

7. Gapes, "The Making of Labour's Defence Policy."

8. Colin Hughes and Patrick Wintour, *Labour Rebuilt* (London: Fourth Estate Ltd., 1990), 3. This is an excellent study of the policy review, and the authors of this Washington Paper have drawn heavily on it.

Chapter 4

1. Hughes and Wintour, *Labour Rebuilt*, 41.

2. National Executive Committee, "An Approach to Policymaking" (Policy Paper), September 1987.

3. Hughes and Wintour, *Labour Rebuilt*, 42.

4. Ibid., 43.

5. Ibid., 46.

6. Britain in the World Group, "Social Justice and Economic Efficiency" (Interim Report), May 1988.

7. Neil Kinnock, speech to a Fabian Conference on "Aims and Values," Central Hall, Westminster, June 17, 1988.

8. Hughes and Wintour, *Labour Rebuilt*, 108–109.

9. Ibid., 110.

10. Ibid., 105–106.

11. Ibid., 107.

12. Ibid.

13. Britain in the World Group, "Social Justice."

14. Ibid.

15. House of Commons Defence Committee, *The Progress of the Trident Programme*, Fifth Report, 1988–1989 session (London: HMSO), June 21, 1989.

16. House of Commons Defence Committee, *The Progress of the Trident Programme*, Third Report, 1987–1988 session (London: HMSO), May 11, 1988, p. XVI.

17. Peter Shore, "Dropping the No-Bomb," *Guardian*, December 28, 1987, p. 13.

18. Ibid.

19. BBC TV, "This Week, Next Week," Neil Kinnock interviewed by Vivian White, June 5, 1988.

20. Peter Jenkins, "The Multilateral Tendency," *Independent*, November 16, 1987, p. 21.

21. Ibid.

22. Ibid.

23. Martin Fletcher and Tim Jones, "Labour Changes Tack on Trident Programme," *Times*, December 15, 1987, p. 2.

24. *Independent*, October 7, 1988.

25. Ibid.

26. Kinnock, "Aims and Values."

27. Campaign Group, "The Campaign for Socialism and the Leadership Election" (pamphlet), March 1988.

28. Hughes and Wintour, *Labour Rebuilt*, 114.

29. Andrew Grice, "Kinnock Triumphant on the Launch Pad," *Sunday Times* (London), May 14, 1989.

30. Reuters, May 9, 1989.

31. Grice, "Kinnock Triumphant."

32. Ibid.

33. Ibid.

34. *Guardian*, May 25, 1989.

35. *Daily Telegraph*, June 30, 1989.

Chapter 5

1. *Meet the Challenge, Make the Change*.

2. Ibid., 83.

3. Ibid., 85.

4. Ibid.

5. Ibid.

6. Ibid., 86.

7. Ibid., 87.

8. *Times* (London), May 17, 1990.

9. *Looking to the Future*, 3.

10. Ibid., 46.

11. Ibid.

12. Ibid.

13. Ibid.

14. Ibid.

15. Ibid., 47.

16. Speech by Neil Kinnock to the Royal United Services Institute, London, January 21, 1991, pp. 1-2.

17. Ibid., p. 4.

18. *Times* (London), April 18, 1990.

19. Ibid.

20. House of Commons, *Official Report* 177, no. 152 (September 7, 1991).

21. "Iraq-Kuwait Conflict," NEC Statement to the 1990 Labour Party Conference.

22. Emergency Resolution to the 1990 Labour Party Conference on the Gulf crisis, proposed by the Fire Brigades Union.

23. House of Commons, *Official Report* 183, no. 38 (January 21, 1991).

24. Minutes of Parliamentary Labour Party Meeting, February 20, 1991.

25. Gavin Strang, "Assault on Hopes of a Credible New World Order," *The Scotsman*, February 16, 1991.

26. Fred Halliday, "The Left and the War," *New Statesman and Society*, March 8, 1991.

27. House of Commons, *Official Report* 193, no. 133 (June 27, 1991).

28. Gerald Kaufman, "Leading the Way to Peace," *Guardian*, July 10, 1991.

Index

115